C000098190

Also available in Sphere Books:

RUGBY JOKES
SON OF RUGBY JOKES
MORE RUGBY JOKES
WHAT RUGBY JOKES DID NEXT
EVEN MORE RUGBY JOKES
RUGBY SONGS
MORE RUGBY SONGS

Rugby Jokes
Score Again

SPHERE BOOKS LIMITED

Sphere Books Limited, 27 Wrights Lane, London W8 5TZ

First published in Great Britain by Sphere Books Ltd 1987
Copyright © E. L. Ranelagh 1987

Set in Baskerville

Printed and bound in Great Britain by
Cox & Wyman Ltd, Reading

Contents

WIMMEN 1
THE RUGBY SONG 11
THE DARING YOUNG MAN ON THE FLYING TRAPEZE 13

SCORING 15
THE PROUD PEDLAR 24
THE MAID OF THE SWEET BROWN KNOWE 27

MARRIAGE 29
WAITING AT THE CHURCH 39

YOU'RE NEVER TOO OLD
AND YOU'RE NEVER TOO YOUNG 41
GAFFER HEPPELTHWAITE 51
THERE DWELT A MAID 53

PROFESSIONS 66
THE DRUMMER 70
THE WOODEN-LEGGED PARSON 79
WE'LL BEAT EVERY BUSH 81

ETHNICS AND NATIONALS 83
MRS MCGRATH 91

IN THE CITY 93
THE MOLECATCHER 105
CAT'S-MEAT NELL 106

IN THE COUNTRY 109
General Guinness 120

ABROAD 123
the Rajah of Astrakhan 136

THE PEARLY GATES, ETC. 137
Beelzebub 145

Rugby Jokes
Score Again

Wimmen

MEANT FOR EACH OTHER

He pursued her, and she encouraged the pursuit. One day he caught her.

'Will you marry me?'

He said these words passionately, and she was all ears. He went on, 'My father is worth three million pounds, and he's now ninety-three years old. When he dies – and it can't be very long now – I shall be very, very rich. What do you say?'

She didn't say. But a week later, she became his mother.

THE FACTS OF LIFE

He: Will you marry me?
She: I'm not very pretty.
He: I'm not bothered – you'll be out at work all day.

MORE FACTS

Dear Harry,

Since our silly quarrel last week I've been unable to sleep or eat. It was my fault entirely, but I do hope you can find it in your heart to forgive me. Giving you back your engagement ring was the stupidest thing I've ever done in my life.

There will never be anyone else for me. Please come back to me, my own true love.

Yours in hope,
Betty.

P.S. Congratulations on winning the Football Pools.

WHY NOT INDEED?

She: Will you still love me when my hair has turned grey?
He: I sure will! I don't see why not. After all, I've loved you when it was red, yellow, brown, black, silver and orange.

RIGHT! WHY?

'Darling, am I the first man you ever kissed?'

'Of course you are the first man I've ever kissed! Why do all you men ask the same silly question?'

2

NEWS

He was driving back from a Sunday afternoon session in the country when he was suddenly struck by a worrying thought.

'I say,' he said, 'you don't tell your mother everything, do you?'

'Oh, no,' she replied. 'My mother couldn't care less; it's my husband who's always asking questions.'

POPPING THE IMPORTANT QUESTION

'Darling, it's true that I'm not good-looking like George Thompson, and I haven't got a good job and a big income like him, or a sports car and a yacht and a villa in the south of France – and I certainly don't have a millionaire for a father like he has – but I do love you very much and I want to marry you. Well, dearest darling, what do you say?'

'Where does George Thompson live?' she asked thoughtfully.

WRONG!

A rather glamorous lady entered the police station and made her way to the enquiry desk.

'I've lost my husband,' she said softly. 'Can you find him for me?'

'Can you give me a description, ma'am?' asked the desk sergeant.

'Certainly! He's six feet, three inches, has broad shoulders, a slim waist, he has curly blond hair and a handsome face, bright blue eyes that seem to see right through you – '

A constable broke in just then. 'Wait a minute, Sarge – I know this woman's husband. It's old Harry Hutchins from the Rose and Crown. He's not in the least like the description she's giving him!'

'I know,' said Mrs Hutchins bitterly. 'But who wants *him* back?'

AN ALL-PURPOSE SUGGESTIVE AND OFFENSIVE REJOINDER FOR MANY AN INNOCENT PHRASE:

'That's what *she* said.'

Try these:

'This is far too long.'
'That's what *she* said.'

'I don't want to take all night.'
'That's what *she* said.'

'Come again soon.'
'That's what *she* said.'

'See if I can get in by the back.'
'That's what *she* said.'

and the all-time classic – same position, no reply:

'Sam, the ceiling needs painting.'

ANOTHER?

This is my first affair,
So what goes where?

TACT?

Secretary to boss: 'I have some good news and some bad news.'
Boss: 'I can't take any bad news today: what's the good news?'
Secretary: 'You're not sterile.'

THE TRUTH

Generally speaking, women are.

RIGHT!

A boy took his girl to a baseball game. She didn't know anything about baseball and very little about any other game, for that matter.

The spectators went wild! The first man at bat hit the ball over the fence for a home run. They went wild over the second batter too – he smashed a line drive for a home run. The third man at bat did the same thing. The stadium rocked with cheers and yells.

Seeing all this, the girl screamed like all the others. She turned to the boy and said, 'Isn't the pitcher wonderful? No matter how the other team holds the bat, he hits it!'

QUEERIES

A man who had been a transvestite for many years had at last made up his mind to become a woman. He went to his doctor and told him of his decision.

But the doctor was not encouraging. He said he did not think any quick action should be taken. This was a very serious matter.

'Give it a good deal more thought,' he said, 'before you make up your mind. It will be an extremely painful operation.'

'You mean the implantation of breasts?'

'No, no, not that.'

'The changing of private parts?'

'No, not that.'

'What then could it be?'

'The shrinking of your brain and the stretching of your mouth.'

FORGIVENESS

Striding along the platform at a country station, a very angry young lady demanded to see a railway policeman straight away. When he came, she pointed to a young man on the platform who, she said, had tried to accost her.

'Now then, sir,' said the policeman to the young man, 'have you been making a nuisance of yourself with this lady?'

'Oh, I hope not!' he said. 'You see, I've just come here to meet my flatmate's girl. He couldn't get here so he asked me to meet her – and I've never actually seen her. But he said she was madly attractive, with a peaches and cream complexion, divine hair, a dream figure, eyes . . .'

'All right, officer,' said the girl. 'I can see it was a natural mistake for him to make.'

OVER THE GARDEN FENCE

A wife came out of her house into the garden when she saw her pretty next-door neighbour in her garden.

'Oh, Brenda,' she said. 'Would you be a dear and put on your bikini? I'd like to get my husband out to mow the lawn.'

OVER ANOTHER FENCE

Mrs Johnson sobbed as she told her tale of woe to her next-door neighbour. 'I've been to see a solicitor about getting a divorce!'

'But why?' asked the neighbour. 'You've been married for twenty-five years! And you've always been so happy!'

'Not any more. His absentmindedness has finally come between us. Last night he was sitting by the fireside, reading the paper, and I crept up behind him just to kiss him on his bald spot.'

'Yes – go on.'

'Without even looking up from the paper he said. "Stop playing about, darling, and finish those letters I dictated yesterday!"'

IN THE OFFICE

First typist: The boss bought me a mink coat for Christmas.
Second typist: To keep you warm?
First typist: No, to keep me quiet.

Pretty girl: My boss is married, but I let him buy me a fur coat. Do you think I did wrong?
Friend: Well, dearie, you didn't do bad.

The bank robbers told the staff that they wouldn't get hurt if they lay face down on the floor. They all complied with this order, except the dumb typist who lay face upwards.

'The other way,' whispered her friend. 'It's a bank raid, not an office party.'

WHAMMY!

A fellow lived on the second floor of a hotel. One evening he was having a few drinks of gin in the town pub when a new girl came along. She was drinking gin too. Pretty soon the two of them got to talking. She said it looked kind of vulgar to sit around in pubs, so he bought another bottle and they went up to his room in the hotel.

After a while he said, 'Let's play whammy.'

She said she had never heard of whammy, so how do you do it?

'You just take off your clothes,' he said, 'and one stands at one side of the room and the other stands at the other. Then you run at each other fast as you can and meet in the middle.'

The girl thought that sounded pretty good. 'Seems like a fun game,' she said, 'let's try it once, anyhow.'

They were pretty drunk by that time, so the fellow ran fast, missed the girl, and fell out of the window.

But he fell into some bushes and didn't get hurt. His trouble was that he was stark naked and there was no way to get back to his room without passing plenty of hotel guests.

So he went to the kitchen door and told the hotel porter to get him a raincoat or something. But the porter said there was no need to do that.

'Jesus Christ! What do you mean!' cried the naked man. 'You think I'm going to walk through the hotel starkers with all the people looking at me?'

The porter repeated that it would be all right. 'Don't worry. Nobody will see you.'

The fellow looked through the door. Sure enough, the lobby was empty and so was the dining-room. He couldn't figure out where the people were because it was only nine o'clock. So he asked the hotel clerk.

'Oh,' said the clerk, 'they're all upstairs. They're watching the doctors trying to get some woman off a doorknob.'

10

THE RUGBY SONG

If I were to marry a man,
And thank the Lord I'm not, sir,
The only man that I would wed
Would be a Rugby hooker.

   For he'd hook balls and I'd hook balls
   And we'd hook balls together:
   We'd be bright in the middle of the night,
   Hooking balls together.

If I were to marry a man,
And thank the Lord I'm not, sir,
The only man that I would wed
Would be a Rugby prop, sir.

   For he'd hold it up and I'd hold it up
   And we'd hold it up together;
   And we'd be bright in the middle of the night
   Holding it up together.

If I were to marry a man,
And thank the Lord I'm not, sir,
The only man that I would wed
Would be a Rugby lock, sir.

   For he'd screw the scrum and I'd screw the scrum
   And we'd screw the scrum together;
   And we'd be bright in the middle of the night
   Screwing the scrum together.

If I were to marry a man,
And thank the Lord I'm not, sir,
The only man that I would wed
Would be a Rugby half, sir.

For he'd put it in and I'd put it in
And we'd put it in together;
And we'd be bright in the middle of the night
Putting it in together.

If I were to marry a man,
And thank the Lord I'm not, sir,
The only man that I would wed
Would be a Rugby back, sir.

For he'd kick hard and I'd kick hard
And we'd kick hard together;
And we'd be bright in the middle of the night
Kicking hard together.

If I were to marry a man
And thank the Lord I'm not, sir,
The only man that I would wed
Would be a referee, sir.

For he'd blow hard and I'd blow hard
And we'd blow hard together;
And we'd be bright in the middle of the night
Blowing hard together.

If I were to marry a man
And thank the Lord I'm not, sir,
The only man that I would wed
Would be a Rugby fan, sir.

For he'd come again and I'd come again
And we'd come again together;
For we'd be bright in the middle of the night
Coming again together.

THE DARING YOUNG MAN ON THE FLYING TRAPEZE

Oh, the girl that I loved she was handsome,
I tried all I knew her to please.
But I couldn't please her a quarter as well
As the man on the flying trapeze.

> *Chorus:* *Oh, he flies through the air with the greatest of ease,*
> *This daring young man on the flying trapeze.*
> *His figure is handsome, all the girls he can please,*
> *And my love he has stolen away.*

Last night as usual I went to her home.
There sat her old father and mother alone.
I asked for my love and they soon made it known
That she-e had flown away.

She packed her box and eloped in the night
To go-o with him at his ease.
He lowered her down from a four-storey flight
By means of his flying trapeze.

He took her to town and he dressed her in tights,
That he-e might live at his ease.
He ordered her up to the tent's awful heights,
To appear on a flying trapeze.

Now she flies through the air with the greatest of ease,
This daring young girl on the flying trapeze,
Her figure is handsome, all boys she can please,
And my love has been stolen away.

Once I was happy, but now I'm forlorn,
Like an old coat that is tattered and torn,
Left to this wide world to fret and to mourn,
Betrayed by a maid in her teens.

13

Scoring

THE GRAFFITI PAGE, TYPED FOR YOUR CONVENIENCE – FROM OURS.

Sex is bad for one . . . but very good for two.

Graffiti should be obscene but not heard.

What does A.I.D.S. stand for?
Anal Injected Death Sentence.

What does GAY stand for?
Got AIDS Yet?

What is pink and hard in the morning?
The *Financial Times* crossword.

Born Free. (Her father was a doctor.)

Jesus is coming! If he remembers to change at Darlington.

Oedipus – call your mother!

What is a eunuch?
A guy cut out to be a bachelor.

Don't vote – it only encourages them.

Don't look for jokes on the walls. The biggest one is in your hand.

ELEMENTARY EDUCATION

Oh innocent lovers of Cupid,
Pray listen to this little verse.
To let a fool kiss you is stupid,
But to let a kiss fool you is worse.

HIGHER EDUCATION

There were rumours of immoral goings-on among the students at a university. This was presently discussed at a meeting of the faculty, who decided that the first thing to do was to establish whether or not the stories were true. A young professor was assigned the job of finding out.

He arranged to be invited to a weekend student party. He arrived early and stayed late. By that time the party had been going on for several hours, and he was very relieved that there had not been a single incident. He said goodnight and went up to bed.

He had not fallen asleep when his door opened. A beautiful female undergraduate appeared, wearing only a flimsy nightie.

'Did you want me?' he asked in surprise.

'Not especially,' she said. 'I just drew you.'

MORE HIGHER EDUCATION, OR MORE MAY BALLS?

In Cambridge, they say the trees along the Cam are more sinned against than sinning.

JOURNALESE

A journalist was sued for libel when he described a life peeress in his column as a 'cow'.

He lost the case, but at the end asked the judge a question. 'So in future, I must not call a baroness a cow, is that right?'

'That is correct.'

'But I suppose I could call a cow a baroness?'

'It would be pointless, but not libellous.'

'Thank you, Your Honour,' said the journalist, and he turned to the plaintiff and said, 'Hello, Baroness.'

OFFICESE

Receptionist: I'm sorry, madam, but Mr Walker has gone to lunch with his wife.

The wife: Oh, well, when he comes back will you please tell him his secretary called in to see him?

DAFFYNITIONS

1   Pregnant Sparrow – One who opens her legs for a lark.
2   Adultery – Wrong people doing the right thing.
3   Brassiere – A device for making mountains out of molehills.
4   Kiss – An application at headquarters for a job at base.
5   Kissing – Upper persuasion for a lower invasion.
6   Prostitute – A busy body.
7   Rape – Seduction without salesmanship.
8   Twins – Womb mates who eventually become bosom 'bodies'.
9   Divorce – When two people cannot stomach each other.
10 Virgin – A wisecrack.
11 Pyjamas – An article of clothing placed beside the bed in case of fire.
12 Board of Trade – A bench in the park.
13 Naval Craft – Elastic in panties.
14 Grub Screw – Sex in the lunch hour.
15 Sand Bag – A desert prostitute.
16 Insulated Screw – a W.R.A.C. in gum boots.
17 Metallurgist – A man who can take a look at a platinum blonde and tell whether she is virgin metal or just a common ore.
18 Love – A fellow feeling.
19 Jealousy – Another fellow feeling.
20 Puff Adder – A man who farts in the bath and counts the bubbles.
21 Alimony – The screw you get for the screw you got.
22 Taxidermist – A man who mounts animals.
23 Papoose – Consolation prize for taking a chance on an Indian blanket.

24 Blunderbuss – A vehicle which takes single girls to the maternity home.
25 Blunderbuss – A coach full of bastards.
26 Egyptian Virgin – A goat that can run faster than an Arab.
27 Ball Race – A tom cat with twenty yards on the vet.

QUEERY?

The middle-aged wife looked moodily at her husband, buried deep behind the *Financial Times* at the breakfast table. She rattled her cup and saucer to try to attract his attention.

'What would you say,' she asked in a loud voice, 'if I were to tell you I was having an affair with your best friend?'

Turning unconcernedly to the closing-prices page, he replied – 'I'd say you were a lesbian.'

QUEERIES

There was a very smart stud rooster in the barn, who had a harem of twenty hens.

When he was getting old, he overheard Farmer Brown saying that he would have to find a new stud.

The rooster started planning his strategy.

Some weeks later, a two-year old rooster walked out of a crate.

The old rooster said, 'I bet you think you're king of the roost.'

'Yes.'

'Let's race for it. If you win, I'll leave. If I win, you leave.'

'OK.'

The hens set the course. The old rooster races. He looks behind and sees the young one just taking it easy.

The race continues. The same thing happens.

Once again, and it's the finishing lap. The young rooster is gradually catching up. He catches up!

But then, the sound of a shotgun, and the young rooster falls. There is Farmer Brown.

He says, 'That's the fifth poof rooster I bought this month!'

QUEERIES?

There was a young student at John's,
Who attempted to fondle the swans.
Whereupon said the porter,
'Oh pray take my daughter!
The swans are reserved for the dons.'

ODDS

In his new neighbourhood, Henry brings his dog with him to the local pub. After a drink or two, he announces that his dog can talk. 'How much do you want to bet?' he asks the crowd.

The barman puts down five.

The dog says nothing and Henry loses.

After another couple of drinks, Henry decides to try again, this time betting a tenner.

The dog doesn't say a word, and Henry beats a hasty retreat.

On the way home he confronts the dog. 'Why the hell didn't you –'

The dog coolly replies, 'Just think of the odds we'll get tomorrow night!'

EVEN!

Two public schoolboys developed a deep dislike for each other, from the start to the end of their school days. Afterwards, they saw nothing of each other till forty years later when they happened to meet at the entrance of one of London's biggest hotels.

One had become an admiral and the other a bishop, but they recognised each other immediately and mutual antipathy radiated as strong as ever.

The bishop was wearing his frock coat, apron and gaiters. The admiral was in full dress uniform with medals, orders and gold lace.

The bishop said to the admiral, 'I say, commissionaire, call me a cab, would you?'

To which the admiral replied, 'Certainly, madam, but should you be travelling in your condition?'

THE CHEMIST

Keen to be on time for his date, Chris stopped at the chemist's shop for a hasty purchase. The chemist gave him a knowing smile, and Chris told him about the lovely chick he met at a party. He was going to spend the evening with her – her parents were going to the opera.

When he got to her house, she and her mother were waiting for her father to get home from work. The father soon walked in, and she introduced Chris.

Chris said, 'Say, why don't Nancy and I join you this evening?'

'You children don't want to spend your evening with us old folks,' said Nancy's mother.

'Sure we do,' said Chris.

'I didn't know you liked opera!' the bewildered Nancy said to her date as he was helping her on with her coat.

'No. And I didn't know your father was a chemist, either,' he said.

YOU KNOW WHAT THAT MAKES YOU

A conceited young man believed he could pick up any girl. It was his way of proving he was God's gift to women.

'Hey, gorgeous!' he called to a pretty girl passing by him on the street. 'Haven't we met before?'

She gave him a look that would have frozen a polar bear.

But this didn't in the least upset him, because he could now come in fast with his crusher.

'My mistake,' he said. 'I thought you were my mother!'

'I can't be,' she replied, 'I'm married.'

SO THAT'S HOW THEY DO IT!

A would-be police officer in the course of examinations was asked how he would go about dispersing a crowd.

'Take a collection,' he answered. 'That works every time.'

SCORING?

'I thought you were taking that wonderful blonde out tonight?'

'I was. We went to the films, then back to her place. We had coffee, chatted for a while, then she lay down on the bed and turned out the light. I can take a hint.'

AFFRONT OR ARREARS

One chorus girl to another: 'His cheque's come back marked "Insufficient fun!"'

A SUMMONS FROM THE POLICE DEPARTMENT

The man who hands you this is a Police Officer. Don't panic. Keep cool. Lie flat on your back and do everything the nice policeman tells you to do.

PRIVATES ON PARADE

Mr Smith hired a new secretary. She was young, sweet and polite. One day while taking dictation she noticed that his fly was open. On leaving the room she said, 'Oh, Mr Smith, did you know your barracks door is open?'

He didn't understand her remark until later on, when he happened to look down and saw that his zipper was unclosed. He decided to have some fun with his new secretary. Calling her in, he asked, 'By the way, Miss Jones, when you saw my barracks door open this morning, did you also see a soldier standing to attention?'

She smiled pleasantly. 'Why no, Mr Smith,' she replied. 'All I saw was a disabled veteran sitting on two old duffle bags.'

THE PROUD PEDLAR

Sweetly sang the nightingale,
And sweetly sang she, O;
But sweeter sang the proud pedlar
As he walked oe'r the lee, O.

'Five hundred pounds into my pack,
Of goods and white monie, O.
And I would give it all,' he said,
'For a night of a gay lady, O.'

A lady lay o'er the castle wall,
Beholding dale and down, O,
And she beheld the proud pedlar
Come singing through the town, O.

'Sing on, sing on, ye proud pedlar,
The song ye sung just now, O.'
'I never sung the song, lady,
But I durst well avow, O.'

'Five hundred pounds into my pack
Of goods and white monie, O,
And I would give it all this day
For a night of a gay lady, O.'

'O where are all my servant maids,
That I pay meat and fee, O?
Go open the gates, pretty Betsy,' she said,
'Let the pedlar unto me, O.

She's taen him by the milk-white hand,
And led him up the stair, O.
Then brought him to her ain chamber,
Where a well made bed was there, O.

He lay there the livelang night
Until the break of day, O;
And turned him at this little wee pack,
When he thought of going away, O.

She's taen the pack into her arms
And diddled it on her knee, O,
'Were it worth as much, and thrice as much,
Ye'd not have a single bawbie, O.'

He stood mourning at the gates,
Till her good lord came hame, O.
Says, 'Who is that stands at my gates,
That makes such noise and din, O?'

'O pity, O pity, kind sir,' he said,
'If any grace can be, O.
O hae some pity, my lord,' he said,
'On a poor pedlar like me, O.'

'I hae travelled along this way
With other pedlars nine, O.
We cast the lots among ourselves,
Who'd gie the rest their dine, O.

The lots gied up, the lots gied down,
And the lots they fell on me, O.
But I had nae mortar to grind my spice,
Till I borrowed it frae your lady, O.

I borrowed your lady's spice mortar,
The pestle it was my own, O.
Now she's kept my pack in pledge of that,
I wadna the truth be known, O.'

He put his hand in his pocket,
And gied her guineas nine, O.
'O take you this, my jewel,' he said.
'It will buy you jewels fine, O.

Ye'll gie the pedlar's pack again,
His pack and his pack pin, O.
Ne'er be too hard for a poor man,
That has his bread to win, O.'

She's taen his pack into her arms
And cast it o'er the wall, O.
And lightly laughed the proud pedlar,
'My pack has gotten a fall, O.

I'll take my pack upon my back,
And I'll sing through the town, O,
That I have cheated a gay lady,
Though my name's but Jamie Brown, O!'

THE MAID OF THE SWEET BROWN KNOWE

Come all ye lads and lassies and listen to me awhile,
And I'll sing for you a verse or two will cause you all to smile;
It's all about a young man, and I'm going to tell you now,
How he lately came a-courting of the Maid of the Sweet Brown
   Knowe.

Said he, 'My pretty fair maid, will you come along with me,
We'll both go off together, and married we will be;
We'll join our hands in wedlock bands, I'm speaking to you now,
And I'll do my best endeavour for the Maid of the Sweet Brown
   Knowe.'

This fair and fickle young thing, she knew not what to say;
Her eyes did shine like silver bright and merrily did play.
She said, 'Young man, your love subdue, for I am not ready now,
And I'll spend another season at the foot of the Sweet Brown
   Knowe.'

Said he, 'My pretty fair maid, how can you say so,
Look down in yonder valley where my crops do sweetly grow,
Look down in yonder valley where my horses and plough
Are at their daily labour for the Maid of the Sweet Brown Knowe.'

'If they're at their daily labour, kind sir, it's not for me,
For I've heard of your behaviour, I have, indeed,' said she.
'There is an Inn where you call in. I have heard the people say,
Where you rap and call and pay for all, and go home at the break of
    day.'

'If I rap and call and pay for all, the money is all my own,
And I'll never spend your fortune, for I hear you have got none.
You thought you had my poor heart broke in talking to me now,
But I'll leave you where I found you, at the foot of the Sweet Brown
    Knowe.'

Marriage

COMFORT

A duke marries a showgirl. Some weeks after the wedding he is shocked to see a life-sized portrait of his wife, completely nude, on display at a Bond Street art gallery.

He is furious with his wife. When he gets home, he tells her so. She snuggles up to him. 'Don't worry about it, sweetie-pie,' she says soothingly. 'He did it from memory.'

COMFORT IN COMPANY

In an exclusive London club, a man found a friend of many years looking miserable.

'What's the matter, old boy? You've had some bad news?'

'It's your wife, old chap.'

'My wife? What about her?'

'I'm afraid she's been unfaithful to us, old thing.'

FIRST THINGS FIRST

Two members of a long-established golf club had just reached the 14th when a funeral procession passed by. One of the players immediately put down his club, removed his hat, and stood solemnly with eyes lowered while the cortege passed by.

As the procession disappeared from view, his friend said, 'Somebody you knew, eh?'

'Yes,' said his friend, replacing his hat and picking up his club. 'And she was a damned good wife to me, too.'

RELATIVITY

Two young society ladies, both unmarried, were taking tea at the Ritz.

'I understand you've been seeing a lot of Lord Zillions,' said one. 'Of course, he's worth a fortune, but don't you think he's a little too old to be considered eligible?'

'My dear,' said the other, 'he's a little too eligible to be considered old.'

WORM'S – EYE VIEW

She was one of the early birds, and I was one of the worms.

GO AWAY!

Once a married woman had a lover. He'd come an' knock on her window. If her husband was out, she'd let him in, but if her husband was there, she'd go to the piano an' play an' sing.

One night he knocked on the window an' the husband was there, so the wife went to the piano and played an' sang:

Go way from the window, my love an' my dove,
Go way from the window, I say.
My babe's at my breast, and the cuckoo's on its nest,
Go way from the window, I say.

The husband heard this an' suspected what was goin' on, so he asked his wife why she didn't sing the rest of the song. She said that was all she knew. So he sat down at the piano an' began peckin' off the tune with one finger an' sang:

Go way from the window, you son of a bitch!
Go way from the window, I say.
For the babe is a-sucking, an' I'll do my own fuckin',
Go way from the window, I say!

MOTHER-IN-LAW

The wedding day finally arrived. The bride's parents had arranged for the reception to be in their home, and after a beautiful church service and a lavish reception party, the young couple were told to go up to their room.

'Oh,' said the bride to her mother, 'let me help you to clear up.'

'No, darling,' said the mother, 'you two go upstairs!'

They went up, and the girl undressed quickly and got into bed. But the groom remained dressed. He said he was too embarrassed.

'Come on, honey,' she said, 'we're in love. There's nothing to be ashamed about!'.

She kept encouraging him, and finally he got into his pyjamas, but he kept his socks on. Only after repeated urgings, did he at last take them off.

Then she screamed!

(It seemed that once an axe had fallen on his foot.)

She ran downstairs to her mother.

'Mother, mother! I'm frightened! He's only got a foot and a half!'

The mother said, 'Ah . . . you stay here and finish the dishes. I'll go up and sort him out!'

MOTHER-IN-LAW

Three sisters were married on the same day. The next morning their mother called them in and questioned them. She asked, 'Which of you has the best husband, and what is the size of his tool?'

The eldest said, 'My husband's is narrow but long.'

'Ah,' replied the mother, 'it's good for the spoon to reach the bottom of the pot.'

The second daughter said her husband's was short but thick.

'It's fine when the peg fits the hole,' answered the mother.

The third said her husband's was short and narrow, 'But he uses it often.'

'And you,' said the mother, 'are lucky to have an income always coming in.'

EH?

Late one night a doctor received a telephone call from a man who said it was very urgent.

'My mother-in-law is lying at death's door. Can you come around at once and pull her through?'

SON-IN-LAW

When things became too much for George, he could hold his tongue no longer. He decided to have a straight talk with his wife.

'Your mother has now been living with us for six years,' he said. 'She's driving me mad. I think it's about time she moved out and found a home of her own.'

His wife stared at him in amazement.

'*My* mother?' she screamed. 'I thought she was yours!'

ANOTHER KIND OF SON-IN-LAW

A strange sight greeted the young wife as she came home. There was her mother standing on a chair with her feet in a bucket of water. She had one finger plugged into the light socket and two wires connected to each side of her head. The hubby was poised by the electricity meter with his hand on the main switch.

'Ah, you're just in time to see Harry cure my rheumatism!' cried the happy mother.

HOW THEY SOLVE THEM IN SCOTLAND

There was an aul' man an' a woman sittin' at the fireside.

The man says, 'Wha's gaun tae mak' the tea?'

The aul' wife says, 'The een that maks up the best song needn't work the nicht.'

So the aul' man, he sings,

> *'Two an' two is four,*
> *Four an' five is nine;*
> *I'll tak a haud o' yer thing,*
> *An' ye'll tak a haud o' mine.'*

'Oh, weel,' she says, 'I've a better een than that.' And she sings,

> *'Two an' two is four,*
> *Four an' five is nine;*
> *I ken the length of your thing,*
> *But ye dinna ken the depth o' mine.'*

An' fairly, the aul' wifie was the smartest an' widna' dae the dishes the nicht!

MARRIAGE ETIQUETTE

Zsa Zsa Gabor was guest expert on a television show dealing with marital problems.

The first question came from a girl. She said, 'I'm breaking my engagement to a very wealthy man who has already given me a sable coat, diamonds, a stove and a Rolls Royce. Miss Gabor, what should I do?'

Zsa Zsa advised, 'Give back the stove.'

Make love, not war!
'I'm married. I do both.'

NATIONAL HEALTH?

An expectant young father was talking to a relaxed veteran father in the waiting room of the maternity ward.

'This is our first child. How long after the baby is born can you resume marital relations with your wife?'

'Well, that depends on whether she's in a ward or a private room.'

MORE WAITING

Two fathers-to-be paced the floor in the waiting-room of the hospital.

'What tough luck,' said one. 'This had to happen during my holiday.'

'You think you have troubles?' said the other. 'I'm on my honeymoon!'

FACTS

A woman was helping her husband pick out a new suit. After much disagreement about it, she finally said, 'Well, go ahead and please yourself. After all, you're the one who is going to wear it.'

'Well, dear,' said the man meekly, 'I figure I'll probably be wearing the jacket and waistcoat anyway.'

MORE FACTS

Two members of an Old Boys club were discussing the permissive society.

'Don't hold with it at all,' said one. 'I certainly never made love to my wife before we were married. Did you?'

'I couldn't say, old boy,' said the other. 'What was her maiden name?'

WARNINGS

A man in love is incomplete until he's married.
  Then he's finished.

Grandchildren don't make a man feel old. It's the knowledge that he's sleeping with a grandmother!

The executive in his fifties was exchanging confidences with a colleague during morning coffee.
  'I was exhausted when I got home last night,' he said. 'And the wife wanted me to take her to the theatre. I reminded her that the factory workers are threatening to walk out on strike, and that I had a full day of negotiations ahead. I told her straight that I was far too tired and had too much on my mind to go to the theatre with her.'
  The other executive, himself a well-married man, nodded sympathetically. Then he asked, 'And what was the show like?'

It's as hard to get a man to stay home after you've married him, as it was to get him to go home before you married him.

WAITING AT THE CHURCH

I'm in a nice bit of trouble, I confess;
Somebody with me has had a game.
But I've still got to keep my single name.
I was proposed to by Obadiah Binks
In a very gentlemanly way;
Lent him all my money so that he could buy a home,
And punctually at twelve o'clock today . . .

There was I, waiting at the church –
Waiting at the church – waiting at the church
When I found he'd left me in the lurch,
Lor, how it did upset me!
All at once he sent me round a note,
Here's the very note,
This is what he wrote –
'Can't get away to marry you today,
My wife won't let me! – let me!'

Lor, what a fuss Obadiah made of me
When he used to take me in the park!
He used to squeeze me till I was black and blue,
When he kissed me he used to leave a mark.
Each time he met me he treated me to port,
Took me now and then to see the play;
Understand me rightly, when I say he treated me
It wasn't him *but* me *that used to pay.*

There was I etc

Just think of how disappointed I must feel,
I'll be off my crumpet very soon.
I've lost my husband – the one I never had!
And I dreamed so about the honeymoon.
I'm looking out for another Obadiah,
I've already bought the wedding ring,
There's all my little faltheriddles packed up in my box –
Yes, absolutely two of everything.

There was I etc.

You're Never Too Old and You're Never Too Young

CELEBRATING

An elderly man was sitting for the afternoon on his customary park bench. A younger acquaintance walking by, paused and greeted him.

Said the elderly man, 'You know, Fred, you ought to do what I do. I don't drink, I don't smoke. I don't overeat. I don't gamble and I don't fool around with women. And you know what? I'm just about to celebrate my eighty-fifth birthday!'

Fred looked at the old chap and said, 'How?'

IT'S A WISE PARENT

Seven-year-old Johnny came home from the park without his new sled.

'An old man and a little boy borrowed it,' he explained. 'They're going to bring it back at four o'clock.'

His parents were upset that he had as good as given away his expensive new gift, but at the same time they were secretly pleased with his kindness and trust.

Four o'clock came – no sled.

But at four-thirty the doorbell rang, and there stood a happy man and boy with the sled and a big box of chocolates.

Johnny suddenly disappeared into his bedroom and then came running out.

'OK,' he said, after examining his sled. 'You can have your watch back.'

THOSE DRIVERS!

A father who didn't see much of his little girl during the week was in the habit of taking her for a drive every Sunday.

One Sunday, however, he had a very bad cold, and rather than disappoint the child, her mother said she would take her instead.

When they returned, the father asked his daughter if she had enjoyed the ride.

'Oh yes, Daddy,' she replied. 'And do you know, we didn't see a single bastard!'

THE CALENDAR OF A YOUNG MAN

A poor boy managed to save enough money to have a woman. He started off into town to find one. On his way he met his grandmother.

'Where are you going?' she asked.

'I'm going into town to get my first piece,' he said proudly, and he twirled his 50p coin.

She exclaimed, 'With all that money? You come on in here!'

THE CALENDAR OF OLD MEN

An old man with waning powers married a young and beautiful girl, and only then realised his own limitations. So he set up a calendar of saints' days on which, out of respect, he and his wife must abstain. Then he found he had to add the holy days of obligation, the four Ember weeks, the eves of the Apostles and even an array of subsidiary saints.

One day he and his wife went on a sea journey. Their boat was boarded by a notorious pirate, who seized the wife and sailed off with her.

And by the time the old man found out where his wife had been taken, she had cheerfully forgotten all the saints' days, and was delighted to find that the calendar didn't apply at sea.

Lord Darnley, ninety years old, sat in the bay window of his ground-floor flat in Park Lane watching the Sunday morning strollers. Suddenly he spotted a pretty *au pair* wheeling a pram to the park.

'Quick, James!' he called. 'My teeth! – I want to whistle!'.

One teenage girl to another: 'I'll never understand men, if I live to be twenty.'

FROM THE SCHOOL YARD

All the teachers at our school go to Church on Sunday
To pray to God to give them strength to whack the kids on
Monday.

Jack and Jill went up the hill
To fetch a pail of water.
Jill forgot to take the pill –
And now she's got a daughter.

Lulu had a baby,
She called it Sunny Jim,
She took it to the swimming baths
To see if it could swim.
It sank to the bottom
And floated to the top
And Lulu got excited
And grabbed it by the
Cockles and mussels two and six a jar
If you do not like them, stick them up your
Ask no questions, tell no lies,
Have you ever seen a policeman doing up his
Flies are a nuisance, fleas are even worse,
And that is the end of Lulu's dirty verse.

What do cannibals play at parties?
Swallow my leader.

What do vampires do every night at 10.30?
Take a coffin break.

What does a male centipede say to a female centipede?
What a lovely pair of legs, legs, legs, legs . . .

There was a young cannibal named Ned,
Who used to eat onions in bed,
His mother said, 'Sonny,
It's not very funny,
Why don't you eat people instead?'

DADDIES

Son: Gee, Dad, why can't I go out in the park and run around like the other boys?
Father: Shut up or I'll nail your other foot to the floor.

Little boy to his father who is taking a shower:
'What are those for, Daddy?'
'Four?'

EQUALISER

Two little boys were in the traditional verbal battle of little boys everywhere.
'My father's better than your father!'
'No, he's not! My father's better than your father.'
'My brother's better than your brother.'
'No, he's not! My brother's better than your brother.'
'My mother's better than your mother!'
'Well, I guess you've got me there. My father says the same thing.'

THE OLD

The Queen was paying a visit to a certain military hospital, and as she walked along the wards she noticed an old soldier lying smartly at attention in one of the beds with his thumbs in line with the seams in his sheets, staring rigidly at the ceiling. The Queen stopped by his bed and said, 'And how are you?'

'I'm doing fine, thank you, Your Majesty,' said the old chap. 'Very gracious of you to ask, Your Majesty.'

'And why are you here?' asked the Sovereign.

'Well, since you ask, Your Majesty,' came the reply, 'I got boils on my botty.'

The Queen gave a faint smile and passed on.

After she had left, the Commanding Officer and the Matron and the staff stormed over to the old man's bed.

'How dare you talk to the Queen like that!' they all said. 'You've disgraced us all – embarrassing Her Majesty in such a stupid way!'

'Well,' said the old man in confusion, 'Her Majesty asked me what was wrong wi' me, so I told 'er!'

The Matron said, 'Yes, but you didn't have to be so specific, did you? You could have just said that you were covered in boils and left it at that. You didn't have to go into the sordid details!'

By coincidence, the Prince of Wales was also due to pay a visit to the same hospital a few weeks later. He was escorted along the same ward and spotted the same old chap lying in the same bed.

He walked over and said, 'How are you today?'

The old soldier, again lying smartly at attention, answered, 'I'm doing fine, Your Royal 'ighness. Very gracious of you to ask, Your Royal 'ighness.'

And then the Prince asked, 'And what is your trouble?'

To which the hapless old man, with the eyes of the Commanding Officer, the Matron, the Ward Sister, all fiercely fixed on him, replied, 'I'm . . . er . . . I'm covered wi' boils, Your Royal 'ighness.'

'Oh, really?' said the Prince. 'So they've spread since my mother was here?'

Advice for your old age: If you can't recall it, forget it.

Old man: 'All this pornography, and me without a pornograph!'

One thing about baldness – it's neat.

BIRDS – HENS FIRST

A man was in trouble with his wife. Whenever she asked him to buy the groceries, he would always stop for a drink on the way home and turn up several hours late – with only half the groceries, and those wilted and soggy.

Well, this one night she was really angry about his forgetting the frying chicken she had sent him for. She yelled at him and told him she wanted a *fresh* frying chicken. 'OK, OK,' he said, and decided he'd go to a poultry farm and pick out a live one.

On the way home from the farm he passed a cinema, and noticed that the film on show was one he wanted to see. But when he went to buy a ticket, the girl at the booth said, 'No way, fella, not with a chicken under your arm!' He turned to go home, and saw from a sign that this was the film's last night. What was he to do?

He went around the corner, stuffed the chicken down the front of his pants, went back and bought a ticket, and then sat down next to two old ladies.

Everything went fine until it began to get warm in the cinema, and the chicken started moving around. He un-zipped his fly a little so that the chicken could stick its head out.

The little old lady next to him elbowed her friend. 'Mildred, Mildred, this man next to me has his thing out!'

'So what? If you've seen one, you've seen them all!'

'Not one like this, Mildred! It's eating my popcorn!'

COCKS

During service on Sunday, a cock flew into the church and perched on a beam. The congregation couldn't see it, but the priest could and it began to interrupt his concentration. Finally he called out,

'Anyone who has a cock should leave!'

The congregation were a bit surprised, but the men began to leave. The priest became even more upset.

'No, no. I mean, anyone who brought a cock into the church must go!'

By now there was only one old man left.

His wife whispered to him, 'Go! Or the priest will think you don't have a cock!'

TISK, TISK! OR TICK-TOCK?

Mother asks little boy what he wants for Christmas.
Boys says: 'I wanna watch.'
Mother says: 'Well, you CAN'T!'

THE BALLAD OF GAFFER HEPPELTHWAITE

Far inland from the lighthouse where the angry tempests rage
Resides old Gaffer Hepelthwaite who drives the Essex stage,
A man of many winters, yet so vigorous withal
That coy spermatozoa still inhabit his left ball.

Alas for Gaffer Hepelthwaite! So virile was his stroke,
So stern and stiff his penis like the mighty Essex oak,
That never yet a maiden did confront his aged e'en
Whose legs he did not yearn to part and place his prong between.

One day the Mayor of Essex town upon his good roan mare
Came riding down the turnpike to enjoy the autumn air,
And with the great official rode his winsome daughter Bess,
Whose passion for fall atmosphere was but a trifle less.

Trot trot along they cantered. Quoth the Mayor, 'Ecod, my lass,
They tell me Gaffer Hepelthwaite can still enjoy his ass.'
'Oh pish!' exclaimed the damosel, and lustily laughed she,
'No fond octogenarian could ever diddle me!'

A rattle interrupted her – a clatter as of feet –
The Essex stage swept into view, the Gaffer in his seat.
'What ho!' the Mayor shouted, 'Pause in your headlong flight.
For here's a pretty argument which you can set aright.'

They made him explanation and without the least ado,
This aged snowy-headed wight his prick brought into view.
The damosel dismounted and the Gaffer climbed on top
And proved the Mayor's contention till that worthy ordered, 'Stop!'

'Stop! did you say, your worship?' said the Gaffer between strokes,
Administering to Bessie five final lusty pokes.
'I pray you, noble gentleman, this order to rescind,
For I find I'm just arriving at my famous second wind.'

'Twas then that Gaffer Hepelthwaite, his penis in the air,
Committed violent outrage on the gentle young roan mare,
And finding that she wearied, next proceeded to engage
The splendid span of animals connected to the stage.

* * *

'Twas twilight over Essex town; the damsel and her sire
In the Mayor's habitation were preparing to retire.
'What cheer, my lass?' the father quoth, and 'Cheer enough,' quoth
she,
'For I shall ride the Essex stage as long as stage there be.'

THERE DWELT A MAID

There dwelt a maid in the Cunny-gate.
  And she was wondrous fair,
And she would have an old man
  Was overgrown with hair.

  And ever she cried, O turn,
  O turn thee unto me.
  Thou hast the thing I have not,
  A little above the knee.

He bought her a gown of green,
  Became her wondrous well,
And she bought him a long sword
  To hang down by his heel.

  And ever she cried, etc.

He bought her a pair of shears
  To hang by her side,
And she bought him a winding-sheet
  Against the day he died.

  And ever she cried, etc.

He bought her a gown, a gown,
  Embroidered all with gold.
And she gave him a night-cap
  To keep him from the cold.

And ever she cried, etc.

He bought her a gown, a gown,
  Embroidered all in red.
And she gave him a pair of horns
  To wear upon his head.

  And ever she cried, etc.

Professions

The Office

SITUATION ADAPTABILITY VALUATION FOR MANAGEMENT PERSONNEL

Choose which you would answer, a or b:

1. You are having lunch with a prospective customer to talk about what could be your biggest sale of the year. During the conversation a blonde walks into the restaurant, and she is so stunning you give your companion a vivid description of what you would do if you had her alone in your motel. She walks over to the table and introduces herself as your client's daughter. What do you do next?

   a)   Ask for her hand in marriage

   OR

   b)   Repeat the conversation to the daughter and just hope for the best.

2.   You are making a sales presentation to a group of corporate executives in the plushest office you've ever seen. Your sphincter suddenly loses control and you break wind in the most convincing manner, causing three water glasses to shatter and a secretary to pass out. What do you do next?

   a)   Offer to come back next week when the smell has gone away.

OR

b)   Challenge anyone in the room to do better.

3.   You are at dinner with a customer and his wife, who looks like a regional runner-up in a Miss World contest. Halfway through dinner you feel a hand on your lap. If you are resourceful you will:

a)   Slip a note to the waiter to have your customer paged and see if the hand goes away when he does.

OR

b)   Excuse yourself and go to the men's room. If he follows you, don't come out until you have a signed order.

4.   You're on your way to see your best account when your zipper breaks and you discover that you forgot to put on your underpants this morning. You decide to:

a)   Call on the customer's secretary instead.

OR

b)   Buy a baggy raincoat and head for the school play-ground.

5.   You've just returned from a trip to Green Bay, Wisconsin. You tell your boss that nobody lives there but whores and football players. He mentions that his wife is from Green Bay. You:

a)   Ask what position she played.

OR

b)   Say, 'So is my fiancée.'

NEW MANAGEMENT COUNSELLING IDEAS?

The boss called one of the clerks into his office and came straight to the point.

'Now look here, White. For the last few weeks your work has become more and more unsatisfactory. You are habitually late for work, and you make book-keeping errors which I wouldn't expect from a sixteen-year-old office boy, let alone a man like yourself who has worked here for fifteen years. What do you have to say for yourself?'

'Well, sir,' replied the clerk, 'I've tried not to let it affect my work, but things haven't been going too well at home, and I'm afraid I've been sick with worry.'

The boss became quite solicitous. 'I'm sorry to hear that,' he said. 'I'm not prying, but if you tell me what's on your mind, perhaps I can help.'

'That's very kind of you, sir, but I don't see how you can help,' said the unhappy one. 'You see, sir, after only two years of marriage, my wife started nagging me about six weeks ago, and it's reached the stage where I'm at my wits' end wondering what to do about it.'

'Ah,' said the boss thoughtfully. 'I think I can help you. In fact I'm sure I can. You see, women need to feel that they are wanted, and you have probably – without realising it – neglected her needs. Take me, for instance; when I get home from work, I embrace my wife and kiss her passionately. Why don't you take the afternoon off and do the same thing? She won't be expecting you, and the element of surprise will make it even better.'

'That's truly kind of you, sir,' said the grateful clerk. 'What's your address?'

THE BOSS'S WIFE

Jill was a very attractive girl who was also an excellent secretary. Her employer's wife, however, considered Jill's appearance an unnecessary hazard and instructed her husband to sack her.

The husband reasoned with his wife that the girl was a competent worker and that he had no wish to lose her. But the wife, who was a director of the company, was adamant.

'If you don't sack her, I will,' she stated finally.

And she did. On hearing the news, Jill grew very angry.

'You're only sacking me because I am better looking than you!' she told the boss's wife. And added, 'I know that I'm better looking than you because your husband told me so.'

The wife made no reply, and Jill made a final crack. 'And I can kiss better than you – so there!'

The wife couldn't contain herself any longer and asked, 'I suppose my husband told you that too?'

'No,' Jill replied sweetly. 'It was your chauffeur.'

IN THE OFFICE

A secretary in a huge office of some fourteen floors was transferred to another part of the building. Her previous boss telephoned her new boss, saying that she was a first-class secretary and that her only vice was gambling!

This seemed rather unusual for a secretary, and the new boss was intrigued. As soon as the girl reported for duty, he called her into his office to question her about it.

'What sort of thing do you bet on?'

'Oh, anything at all,' she replied. 'For instance, I'll bet you £5 that you have a mole on your left shoulder.'

'I'll take that bet,' said the boss promptly. He removed his jacket and shirt to prove that there was no mole there.

The girl shrugged her shoulders, handed over the £5 and left the office.

The boss wasted no time in phoning his colleague, the girl's previous boss.

'I've taught that girl a lesson,' he began, and recounted what had happened.

'You think you won? The girl won!' was the reply. 'Before she left here, she bet me £10 that she'd have your shirt off your back five minutes after she met you!'

Boss: My right hand never knows what my left hand is doing.
Typist: Maybe not – but I do.

'You've had days off already, Hanson, for your mother-in-law's funeral, your little girl's measles, and your boy's christening. What is it now?'

'I'm going to get married, sir.'

IN THE OFFICE?

She was only the Town Clerk's daughter, but she let the borough surveyor.

NOT IN THE OFFICE

A beautiful young socialite visited the studio of a famous painter to ask if he would paint her in the nude. 'I'll pay £1,000,' she said.

He refused, explaining that it was against his principles.

A week later she phoned him and offered him £2,500. Again he refused.

When she called him a third time and offered £5,000, he asked if he could think it over.

The next day, he phoned her and said he'd do it, but on one condition. 'I'll have to wear socks,' he said. 'I need a place for my brushes.'

CERTAINLY NOT IN THE OFFICE

Then there was the reviewer of a film who reported it to the police because of the orgy scene.

The film-maker defended his film by asking, 'What's the matter? Haven't you ever seen seven men, four women and a sheep all madly in love with each other?'

Doctors

IT'S ALL IN THE MIND

When many years ago Queen Marie of Romania made a state visit to America, she was shown through a famous university where the leading American psychiatrist was a professor.

She asked to meet this famous man. The official party duly made its way to his department and she was formally introduced.

'Doctor,' said the university president, 'this is the Queen of Romania.'

'Ah,' said the old professor, 'very interesting. So the old dear thinks she's a Queen, eh?'

FIRST THINGS FIRST

A worried man was talking to a consultant physician about his complaint.

'I seem to have become completely irresponsible. Last year I persuaded my bank manager to give me a £5,000 loan. Then I left home and blew the lot in an orgy on the Riviera. My GP thought that as a last resort I should come to see you . . .'

Doctor (briskly): His name?

Patient: Dr Brownlow.

Doctor: Not your GP's name, you fool! Your *bank manager's*.

ANOTHER CONSULTATION

'It's my husband, doctor,' said the harassed-looking woman. 'You see, he's convinced that he's a washing machine. He just squats in the kitchen, gurgling and rolling his eyes, while he swallows the laundry . . .'

'Precisely what do you want me to do?' asked the doctor.

'Well, you could talk to him or something,' said the woman. 'You see, he's not very good with the woollies.'

NO CONSULTATION

Woman patient: I've got all my clothes off. Where shall I put them?
Psychiatrist: On top of mine.

CURE

A very agitated mother took her son to a child guidance clinic; the child was noisy and aggressive. The psychiatrist, having observed that the boy was hyperactive, made out a prescription for a sedative but forgot to specify who was to take it.

The next appointment was a week later. 'How has your little boy been behaving this week?' the doctor asked.

The mother shrugged. 'Who cares?' she drawled.

CURED

The patient was in the office and the diagnosis was simple. Steve was an introvert, afraid to face the world, unable to say 'Boo' to a duckling.

'What you lack is self-confidence,' said the psychiatrist, 'and one way of getting it is to go to bed with a woman.'

'How can I, doctor?' asked Steve. 'I'm afraid even to look a woman in the face, let alone go to bed with her.'

'Not to worry. Go to this address, tell the woman that I sent you, and she will take care of everything.'

Steve went round to the address, which turned out to be a commercial hotel. When he knocked at the room door, a woman answered, took him inside, gave him a stiff drink and pronto! they were in bed.

Steve called at the doctor's consulting rooms first chance. His head was erect, his shoulders back, there was a spring in his walk and a confident smile on his face. He also had a beautiful black eye.

'I'm cured, doc!' he announced. 'Just look at me – confident, self-assured, happy . . . the complete extrovert!'

'Fine,' said the psychiatrist, 'but what about the black eye?'

'Oh, the woman gave me that. She asked for a fiver. Damned cheek! I told her it was all on the National Health . . .'

ON THE FLOOR

When the floor nurse on Ward C answered the phone, a voice at the other end said, 'Can you tell me, please, how Mr Hunter is getting along?'

'He's doing very well,' she replied. 'I believe he's going home tomorrow. Who shall I say called?'

'This is Hunter. No one tells me a thing around here.'

NEXT APPOINTMENT

Will it be a £25 tune-up or a £500 overhaul?

CONVERSATION AT A COCKTAIL PARTY

'Are you a psychologist?'
'Why do you ask?'
'You're a psychologist.'

PATIENT TO DOCTOR

'My sex-life is no good any more,' the man complained to the doctor.

The doctor examined him. 'You're unfit,' he said. 'I suggest that you jog 5 miles a day. Give me a ring next week and let me know how you're getting on.'

A week later his phone rang.

'Well, how's your sex-life?' the doctor asked.

'How the hell should I know? I'm 35 miles from home.'

DOCTOR TO PATIENT

'I've treated a few cases like yours before, so I should have some kind of luck this time.'

PATIENT TO DOCTOR

'I keep thinking there are two of me, Doctor.'

'OK, tell me again – and this time don't both speak at once.'

DOCTOR TO PATIENT

'I think you ought to stop taking sleeping pills every night,' a doctor warned an ageing telly star. 'They're habit-forming, you know.'

'Don't be silly,' she said. 'I've been taking them every night now for twenty years and they haven't become a habit yet.'

WHO TO WHOM?

'I suffer from loss of memory, Doctor.'
'I see. How long have you had this problem?'
'How long have I had what problem?'

The Military

TWO SKI-TROOPERS

'What's the first thing you're going to do when you get home?'

'Do you have to ask?'

'Well, what's the second thing you're going to do?'

'I'm going to take off these damn skis!'

TRUST NOT IN LUCK

Tom and Dick were both afraid they would be transferred to the Middle East. They were given the same date for the physical examination, so they went to it together.

'I'm worried sick,' said Dick. 'They'll get me, I know.'

'I'm not worried at all,' said Tom. 'You know why? Because I have to wear a truss. They won't want me.'

He was absolutely right. The doctors looked at the truss and waved him off. He came back to Dick, who was still waiting to be examined.

'Look,' he said to Tom, 'can I borrow that thing while they look at me?'

'Sure,' said Tom.

So Dick figured he had the truss and all the right answers when they questioned him.

'What's wrong with you?' they asked.

'Hernia.'

'How long have you been ruptured?'

'Twenty years.'

'Do you take any exercise?'

'No, I can't.'

He eagerly awaited the physicians' verdict.

'You're drafted,' they said. 'If you've been wearing a truss upside down for twenty years, you're ready to go to the Middle East and ride a camel.'

SONG

'In my sweet little Alice-blue gown –
That's why the Marines turned me down.'

SOLDIERS

A soldier asked for home leave because his wife was going to have a baby. When he came back, his officer asked, 'Well, was it a boy or a girl?'

'I don't know. These things take time, you know.'

FRENCH LEAVE TOO?

A sailor on leave went with his girlfriend to the local padre. 'How soon can you marry us?' he asked.

'Well, we have to allow three weeks to elapse before . . .'

'Three weeks! But I've only got a thirty-six-hour pass!'

Then, taking the minister aside he whispered, 'Do you think you could just say a few words to see us over the weekend?'

THE DRUMMER

'Twas in the merry month of May,
When lasses feel so very queer,
Soldiers through the town did stray
   And among the rest a drummer fair.
The ladies flocked, a lively set,
Among the rest was jovial Bet
Who well knew how to do the trick,
And all they wanted was the drummer's stick.

Roger's wife cried to the lad,
   Who beat the drum with such a grace,
'To play with your stick I am half mad,
   So come with me to a certain place.'
The drummer out of the ranks did fall,
Being always ready at roll call,
And in a grove of olives thick
She played with the drummer's magic stick.

The cobbler's wife came next, oh dear,
   And on the grass did quickly fall.
She said that she did feel so queer
   Because the snob had lost his all.
Says the drummer, 'If that is the case,
His awl I quickly can replace.'
He showed it her – says she, 'How thick,
What awl can match a large drum stick?'

The tailor's wife was filled with grief,
  And did her sad lot much deplore.
Her husband, to give her relief,
  Had not used his needle a month or more.
With her the drummer commenced his drumming,
When she beheld her husband coming.
He came upon them in the nick,
And found her having the drummer's stick.

There were three old maids, though fond of fun,
  Declared they'd never had a man.
They to the drummer off did run,
  And said, 'Please us as you only can.'
So he laid them all upon the grass,
Brought forth the magic stick, alas!
They looked at it till fit to burst,
Then had a mill which should have it first.

Lawyers

PRIVATE DETECTING

A private eye was reporting to the boss concerning a shadow job. 'I traced her to Manchester, and then she gave me the slip.'

'Then what?' asked the boss.

'I traced her to Glasgow, and she gave me the slip there too.'

'This is getting monotonous!' said the boss impatiently. 'What happened after that?'

'I traced her to Birmingham, and – '

'She gave you the slip?'

'No, sir. In Birmingham she gave me the bra.'

COUNSEL IF NOT DEFENCE

A very pretty young dolly was in the dock and the defence lawyer was making his final speech to an all-male jury.

'What is to be the fate of this young innocent girl?' he asked with great feeling. 'Her future is in your hands. Is it to be a cold cheerless cell, or her cosy flat at 48, Golden Mansions, Hetherington Street, phone number 488–5794?'

ANOTHER PRIVATE DICK

A wealthy man employed a private detective to check on a girl he'd recently met, because he thought he might want to marry her.

Two weeks later he received the reply: 'The girl in question comes from an excellent family. She has a first-class reputation. She has many friends of high social standing. She was spoken of most highly until a few weeks ago when she began to go out with a business executive of questionable character.'

IT COULD DRIVE A MAN TO MURDER

'It's £100 in your pocket,' whispered the defendant's lawyer to the juror, 'if you can get the jury to bring in a verdict of manslaughter.'

The jury was out for several days, but the verdict finally came – and it was indeed a verdict of manslaughter.

The lawyer thanked the juror warmly as he paid him the money. 'Yes,' said the juror, 'it was hard work, but I got there in the end. All the others wanted an acquittal.'

NICE . . . OR HONEST

The prosecuting lawyer was a bit of a bully. He said sarcastically to a witness who disagreed with him, 'Huh, you're a nice fellow, ain't you?'

'I *am* a nice fellow,' replied the witness. 'If I was not on oath, I'd say the same of you!'

Clergy

LITURGY AND RESPONSE

A policeman stopped a car for speeding. To his surprise, the driver was a clergyman, who started intoning something from the Bible.

'Sorry, Reverend,' said the policeman, 'what you say won't change anything. Your speedometer runneth over.'

PRECOCIOUS

Three rather elderly clergymen were having tea together one afternoon. By some quirk, conversation turned to their most embarrassing moments.

When it came to the turn of the third member of the group, he told how his mother had caught him looking through a crack in the bathroom door while the maid was taking a bath.

The other two chuckled. 'Yes,' said one, 'we certainly got up to some tricks in our youth.'

'What are you talking about?' asked the third cleric. 'This was yesterday!'

DADDY SHOULD KNOW

The vicar's wife was entertaining some small children. Turning to a little girl, she said, 'I understand God has sent you a little baby brother.'

'Yes,' said the little girl. 'And He knows where the extra money's coming from too. I heard Daddy say so.'

CLERGY AGAIN

Two curates were talking. One asked, 'How do you get on with the young ladies in your parish?'

The other replied, 'I seek safety in Numbers. How about you?'

'I take refuge in Exodus.'

ONE OF OURSELVES!

A new vicar moved into a small country parish, and it soon became apparent to him that the community did not accept him. His congregation was very small, and everyone ignored him when they passed him in the street.

He thought the best way of getting acquainted would be to visit the local pub and buy a couple of rounds for everyone.

However, to his disappointment, the locals refused his offer and he was left to sit by himself in a corner. After a while he got up and went to the gents, where he was amazed to see a big picture of a beautiful girl, clad only in a fig-leaf, on the wall.

When he returned to his seat he was delighted to find everybody in a completely different mood. They all welcomed him, and everyone wanted to buy him a drink.

'Well, well!' he exclaimed. 'What a transformation! I come in for a drink and everyone ignores me. Then, not an hour later, I come back from the toilet and get this response! Whatever has happened?'

'Well, Vicar,' said the barman, 'when you lift that fig-leaf, all the lights in the bar go out!'

STREAMLINED CONFESSION

To save time, a priest posted a list of penances in the confessional.

A man came in. 'Forgive me, Father, for I have sinned. I've been with a woman three times.'

The priest said, 'I'll have to fine you. Take a look at the list pinned up over there and you'll see how much.'

The man read out, 'It says, £5 for the Church, £5 for the Holy Water, and £5 for the priest.' So he paid the priest £15 and departed.

Next in line was a woman. She had committed adultery just once, she said. The priest was in a hurry, but she relished telling him about what was, to her, a novel detail.

The priest heard her out. When she had finished he said, 'Read the list.'

She did.

He said, 'But that will be £20 – £5 added to the £15. As above.'

NEIGHBOURLY

A rabbi had the misfortune to run his car into the side of Father Murphy's car. He jumped out straight away and ran to Father Murphy who was still sitting in the driver's seat, looking a bit pale.

The rabbi was loud with apologies. 'My dear Father Murphy, how sorry I am! That I should be so silly as to do this to you of all people, a fellow man of God! Are you all right?'

'Oh, yes, no injuries, Rabbi,' said the priest, 'but I am a bit shaken up.'

'Of course you are,' said the rabbi with great concern. 'Here – have a sip of this; it's good whisky!' And he handed a hip flask to the priest who thanked him and drank heartily.

'Go on, Father, have another! It's all my fault. Drink deep! Don't worry about the cost.'

Father Murphy needed no second bidding and took another deep swig.

'Won't you have one, Rabbi?' he asked.

'With the police arriving already?' exclaimed the rabbi.

THE WOODEN-LEGGED PARSON

A barber there was named Timothy Briggs,
Quite famous for making good wigs,
Till with a lass, named Becky Bell,
Slap over the ears in love he fell.

So they went to the church the knot to tie,
To the wooden-legged parson, Jonathan Sly,
If you'd seen him, I'm sure, you'd have laughed at him, plump
As he mounted the pulpit stairs with a thump.

They'd only been married a week or two,
When Becky turned out a most terrible shrew.
'No comfort I have with this woman,' he said.
'So I'll go back to the parson and get unwed.'

So he went to the parson and said, 'Mr Sly,
If I live with this woman I surely shall die.
You know, sir, you made us two into one,
So I'm come to know if I can't be undone.'

The parson said, 'This is a thing rather new.
I don't know that I have power my flock to undo.
But in hope that you'll lead a more happy life,
I'll call at your house and admonish your wife.'

The barber quite pleased went taking his glass,
And the parson stumped off to lecture the lass,
When the barber went home, laws, what did he see,
But the parson with Becky a-top of his knee.

The barber at this bristled every hair,
Says he, 'Mr Sly, what are you doing there?'
'Why, you know that you wanted undoing, my man,
So you see I am trying as hard as I can.'

'Yes, I think I'm undone as I never was before!'
So he kicked Mr Parson straight out of the door.
There he lay in the street, and his wooden leg stood
Like a spade sticking up in a cart-load of mud.

They lived after this rather more reconciled,
And in nine months from then she brought forth a child.
But the barber he hung himself up on a peg,
When he found the child born with a new wooden leg.

WE'LL BEAT EVERY BUSH

The gentry to the King's Head go,
*   The nobles to the Crown,*
The knight you'll at the Garter find,
*   And at the Plough the clown.*

*   But we'll beat every bush, boys*
*   In hunting of good wine,*
*   And value not a rush, boys,*
*   The landlord or his sign.*

The bishop to the Mitre goes,
*   The sailor to the Star,*
The parson topes beneath the Rose,
*   At the Trumpet, men of war.*

*   But we'll etc.,*

The bankrupt to the World's End roams,
*   No fair the Feather scorns,*
The lawyer to the Devil runs,
*   The tradesman to the Horns.*

*   But we'll etc.,*

Ethnics and Nationals

NORTH OF THE BORDER

In Northern Ireland a few years ago, a Roman Catholic priest decided to hold a Sunday School for all faiths, so the local Protestant children were duly invited. A Jewish boy came along too.

The priest asked them, 'Who was the most holy man in history?'

A Catholic boy waved his hand.

'Yes?' the priest nodded to him.

'Saint Peter,' said the boy.

'You're nearly right, you're nearly right,' said the priest, 'but not quite.'

A Protestant boy waved his hand. 'The Prime Minister?' he asked.

'No!' replied the priest. 'You're miles away!'

The Jewish lad waved his hand. 'Saint Patrick,' he said.

'Well done!' said the priest. 'Well done. How did you know?'

'Well,' said the boy, 'it's really Moses, but business is business.'

AND SOUTH

An Englishman took an estate in Ireland for the summer. One day he brought his dog out for a walk and met one of the local villagers coming in the opposite direction.

'Bedad, that's a wonderful animal you have there, sorr,' said the local. 'Now what kind of dog would that be?'

'It's a cross between a monkey and an Irishman,' said the Englishman with a smile.

'Is that a fact now?' said the local. 'So it's related to both of us then!'

The Englishman's wife had an encounter, too. She decided she should see something of the countryside and hired a local to drive her around.

As they set out, he began to point out places of interest, but she silenced him. 'I hired you to drive, not to talk.'

He kept silent for the rest of the trip, but when he handed her his bill she noticed he'd charged an extra £5.

'What is this item for?'

'Ah, well now, that's for cheek, ma'am. I don't usually take it, but when I do, I charge for it.'

USA

Rastus was cleaning a window on a high floor of a skyscraper when his safety-belt gave way. He barely managed to grab the window-sill and he hung there by his hands, yelling for help.

'Oh Lawd!' he cried, 'Ah'm not yet ready for dem Pearly Gates an' dem golden slippers! Save me!'

Suddenly he saw a figure flying towards him from the sky. As it got closer he saw it was an angel.

'Hi there, Rastus,' said the angel. 'Have you got faith in the Lord?'

'Ah shure do, Ah shure do!'

'Then I will help you,' said the angel, 'I will teach you how to fly. Now show your faith, just take one hand off the window-sill.'

'Oh, Ah cain't do that, Ah cain't!'

'Yes, you can, Rastus. Show your faith.'

Sobbing with fear, Rastus closed his eyes and slowly let go with his left hand. It took all his effort to hold on with the right.

'Good, Rastus. Well done. And now I want you to let go with your other hand.'

'Lawd, no, Ah cain't,' sobbed Rastus.

'You can do it, Rastus. Have faith! Praise the Lord, and let go!'

So Rastus let go.

He hurtled downwards and smashed to death on the pavement below.

The angel flew away smiling. 'Never did like niggers, no-how,' he said.

REDSKINS

The Lone Ranger and Tonto were in the middle of the desert in the sweltering heat when they were suddenly surrounded by 50,000 Indians on the warpath.

'Tonto, I think this could be the end for us.'

'What do you mean, "us", pale-face?'

SQUELCHEES?

At a diplomatic luncheon a young Englishman found himself seated next to a Chinese. Wishing to be friendly, after soup had been served he turned to him and said, 'Likee soupee?'

The Chinese merely smiled, and the Englishman thought, 'Poor fellow, he doesn't understand English.'

When the meal was over, there were some speeches. The Englishman was aghast when the Chinese rose and replied to the toast with a polished speech of wit and epigram in perfect English.

As he sat down to applause, he turned to the Englishman and said, 'Likee speechee?'

UP THE IRISH

It was a needle match between Dublin and Belfast, played at the biggest ground in Dublin.

The first goal was scored by the home team, and an Englishman in the crowd cheered along with the home supporters until he saw a big fellow from Belfast giving him a black look.

Then Belfast scored, and the Englishman, with half an eye on the Belfast man, decided he'd better cheer with the visiting supporters. But now he attracted the attention of a bunch of ugly-looking customers from the Dublin fans.

It went like that throughout the match. Whichever side scored, the frightened Englishman cheered.

At last the Irishman standing next to him could take it no longer. Grabbing him by the scruff of the neck, he shouted, 'What's the matter with you, man? Have you no religion at all?'

A SPENDTHRIFT

A Scotsman won a yacht in a lottery, but instead of looking happy, had the longest face in the room. A friend asked him why.

'Well, ye see, I bought twa tickets, an' I canna see what possessed me to buy the second one.'

POMS

Grow your own dope. Plant a Pom.

PERSIANS

A remarkable race are the Persians,
They have such peculiar diversions,
*   They make love by day,*
*   In the usual way,*
And save up the night for perversions.

FRENCH

A Frenchman was in despair while trying to learn English.
The final straw was when he read: '*Oklahoma!* pronounced
success.'

NATIONALISTS

A Scotsman in London was talking to an American tourist. 'And tae what country do ye belong?' he said.

'To the greatest country in the world!'

'Mon, so do I!' said the Scot. 'But ye dinna talk like a Scotsman!'

JUNE 21st

An Englishwoman will say it's the longest day of the year. A Frenchwoman will say it's the shortest night.

VOLTAIRE IN ENGLAND

When he visited England in the 1770s, Voltaire's carriage was recognised by an angry crowd in London. They started shouting, 'Hang him! Hang the cursed Frenchman!'

But they applauded and laughed when Voltaire called out, 'Am I not punished enough by not being English?'

WALL

A Christian was visiting Jerusalem and his Israeli friend took him to see the Wailing Wall. The Christian put on a hat and said, 'Thank you, Lord, for all the blessings you have bestowed on me.'

Then he turned to his friend. 'Is that what one says here?'

'That's right,' said the Israeli, smiling.

The Christian turned to the Wall and said, 'Please, Lord, keep my family and friends in good health and prosperity.'

He turned to the Israeli again. 'Is that right?'

'That's right.'

'And persuade the Israelis to see the error of their ways and to give back to the Arabs the land taken from them in recent conflicts, so that there may be peace in the Middle East. Is that right?'

'You're talking to a wall.'

MRS McGRATH

'Oh, Mrs McGrath!' the sergeant said,
'Would you like to make a soldier out of your son, Ted,
With a scarlet coat and a big cocked hat,
Now Mrs McGrath, wouldn't you like that!'

Chorus:
  With a too-ri-ay, too-ri-ay, whack-fol-the diddle with a too-
ri-ay.

So Mrs McGrath lived on the sea shore
For the space of seven long years or more,
Till she saw a big ship sail into the bay,
'Here's my son Ted, wisha clear the way!'

Chorus

'Oh Captain dear, where have you been,
Have you been sailing on the Mediterreen,
Or have ye any tidings of my son Ted,
Is the poor boy living or is he dead?'

Chorus

Then up comes Ted without any legs,
And in their place he has two wooden pegs.
She kissed him a dozen times or two,
Saying, 'Holy Moses, 'tisn't you!'

Chorus

'Oh were ye drunk or were ye blind
When ye left yer two fine legs behind?
Or was it walking upon the sea
Wore ye two fine legs from the knees away?'

Chorus

'Oh I wasn't drunk and I wasn't blind
When I left my two fine legs behind,
For a cannon ball on the fifth of May
Swept my two fine legs away.'

Chorus

'Oh then me boy,' the widow cried,
'Yer two fine legs were yer mammy's pride!
Them stumps of a tree won't do at all;
Why didn't ye run from the cannon ball?'

Chorus

'All foreign wars I do proclaim
Between Don Juan and the King of Spain,
And by heaven I'll make them rue the time
That they swept the legs from a child of mine.'

Chorus

'Oh then, if I had you back again,
I'd niver let ye go fight the King of Spain,
For I'd rather my Ted as he used to be
Than the King of France and his whole Navee.'

Chorus

In The City

YOU CAN'T WIN

One secretary to another as they eye a giant computer, 'It replaced twenty-five men – darn it!'

OR CAN YOU?

A salesgirl to a voluptuous customer trying on a revealing dress, 'It's purposely made a little daring for office wear – it's designed to make the boss think twice before installing automation.'

POOFTER-WOOFTER

A queer, dressed in a flowered blouse, carrying a handbag and wearing high heels, was walking his dog in the city. He minced into a pub and said to the barman, 'Could I have a gin and tonic please, sweetie?'

The barman says, 'I'm sorry, but we don't serve people like you.'

The queer says, very slowly, 'Look, sugar-lips, pour me a gin and tonic, please.'

'I said, we don't serve people like you.'

'Now look, sweetie, if you don't let me have a gin and tonic, I'll set my guard-dog on you.'

'Sorry, can't serve you.'

So the queer says, 'Sic him, Pinkie!'

And Pinkie leaps on to the bar, pins the barman against the shelves, and says, 'Bowsie, wowsie!'

EXCLUSIVE

Two retired colonels were talking in their Piccadilly club.

'Did you hear about old Ponsonby?' asked one.

'No. What about him?'

'He's been cashiered from the Horse Guards. They found him screwing his mount.'

'Good Lord! Was it a stallion or a mare?'

'A mare of course. Ponsonby's no pervert!'

BOOK TITLES IN A SOHO SHOP

The African Maid by Erasmus B. Black.
The Two Happiest Men in the Navy by John FitzPatrick and Patrick FitzJohn
The Tiger's Revenge by Claude Balls
The Easiest Way by Eileen Back
The Chinese Pervert by 'Peking' Tom.

TIME OFF FOR FUN OR GAMES

An elderly man walked into a large firm and asked to see the office manager.

'Yes, sir?'

'My name is Bartlett. My grandson is an office boy here. I'm up in London to take him to a football match, if you could let him have the afternoon off.'

'I'd like to help,' said the office manager, 'but I'm afraid he's already been given the afternoon off to go to your funeral.'

BUSINESS SECTION

A small van loaded with glassware was trying to back into a narrow gateway, but the driver couldn't manage it, and the van crashed into one of the gate-posts, smashing most of the load to slivers.

The driver jumped out to examine the damage. As a crowd gathered, he seemed almost in tears. A kindly old man said to him, 'Will you have to make good the damage out of your own pocket?'

'I'm afraid so.'

'Dear me, dear me!' said the old chap. 'I'll tell you what I'll do.' And he took off his hat and put a pound into it. 'I'll take up a collection – I'm sure some of these good people will help you out too.'

And the old gent managed to collect a respectable sum from the crowd, which had grown to quite a size. The cash was handed over, and the old chap hailed a cab and departed.

Looking after the disappearing taxi, the driver said, 'That's what I call a really sharp operator.'

'Why do you say that?' asked one of the donors.

'He's my boss.'

AT THE ROYAL ACADEMY

A tourist was walking around the Summer Exhibition. He moved round quickly, apparently finding nothing worth looking at.

Pointing to a large frame, he sneered to the attendant, 'I suppose this monstrosity is what you call modern art?'

'No sir,' said the attendant, 'we call it a mirror.'

SLOW BOATS

A sailor on leave in London picked up a beautiful young South American girl, who told him she was homesick and desperate to return to her family. But she had no money for the fare, and was so miserable that she was thinking of ending it all by jumping into the Thames.

'No, don't do that, love,' said the sailor. 'I'll tell you what – my ship's sailing for Brazil tomorrow. Why don't we smuggle you aboard? You can stay in my cabin. Mind you, you won't be able to come out, and it will take six weeks to get to Rio. And there's only one bunk . . . '

The girl was so grateful for the sailor's help that she agreed to his plan at once.

So for the next few weeks, the sailor had the time of his life. Working all day and loving all night was idyllic! Until the Captain decided to make a thorough search of every corner of the ship.

It was not long before the girl was discovered. The Captain demanded to know why she was in the sailor's cabin. The girl told him of her great desire to reach her homeland, and the Captain replied, 'My dear, I have a nasty shock for you. This is the Woolwich ferry.'

SMART DOG

A man was very proud of his terrier, whom he considered the smartest dog he'd ever owned – except for one thing. No matter how often the terrier was punished, he could not be house-broken. Time after time, he widdled on the chairs and sofa in the sitting-room.

One day the man decided this bad habit must end. He took the terrier to the park, and peed against a tree to show the dog what to do. The dog watched with alert interest.

Back home, the man waited to see if the dog had learned. Sure enough, he had. The terrier got up on his hind legs, held himself in his paws, and on the same chairs and sofa, did it like a man.

A NEWCASTLE PUBLIC NOTICE, 1782

Be aware of Pick-Pockets in a Crowd. If you are jostled up on one Side, look sharp out on the other, first seize the Thief on the Pocket-Side, then the Jostler on the other, and also the Marcher off, and carry them before a Magistrate to be examined. If the Offenders are not easily to be taken, call the Assistance of the People present to stop the Thieves.

IN ANY CITY

A pretty girl was crying as she talked with a girl friend.

'Why, Alice!' said the friend. 'Are you weeping because Tom Keys has married Lizzie? I suppose you wish he'd have had you?'

'No,' sobbed the other. 'That isn't it. I wish he hadn't.'

SOHO?

Did you hear about the stripper who was so ugly that when she took her clothes off, the audience started shouting, 'Put 'em on! Put 'em on!'

SOHO!

A not-so-young lady, very upset, demanded to see the cinema manager during the interval.

'Are you the manager?'

'I am. Is anything wrong?'

'I should say there is! During the first film I had to move my seat three times!'

'I'm sorry to hear that, madam. Why? Were you being interfered with?'

'Yes!' she said, '. . . eventually.'

DEFINITION OF A GENTLEMAN

A man who is the product of six generations of good breeding, or one good guess at the stock market.

DEFINITION OF A BUSINESSMAN

A beggar approached an affluent city gent in the street and asked for a handout.

'Certainly not!' replied the gentleman. ' I never hand out money to anyone in the street.'

'What do you want me to do then?' asked the beggar. 'Open an office?'

GRAFFITI IN THE CITY

I am a mistake – legalise abortion.

This week I'm going with Bill but I like Jim – Alice.
(A week later):
This week I'm going with Jim but I like Bill – Alice.
(And the week after that):
This week we are not going with Alice – Bill and Jim.

In a pub:
You don't buy beer here. You just rent it.

On a wall covered with obscenities:
This wall will soon appear in paperback.

I love grils!
(In another handwriting): It's not grils, stupid, it's girls.
(Third handwriting): What about us grils?

BUSINESS SCHOOL

Term I   Introduction to Nose-picking
Term II   Abnormal Nose-picking
Term III   Applied Nose-picking
Term IV   Individual Nose-picking Differences
Term V   Introduction to Plastic Surgery.

CITY UNIVERSITY

GVMT 100	Political Theory: Machiavelli to the Corner Grocer
PHIL 110	How to Ask Lots of Questions and Appear Intelligent. Text: Plato as taught by Socrates
SPEECH 310	Political Speechmaking through Use of the Buzz Phrase Generator
BUS 400	Ambiguous Bills
ECON 410	Use of GNP as Index of National Wealth and Other Jokes
LAW 480	Torts and other Bitches.

AT A TRADE CONFERENCE

Two businessmen met at a conference.

'Tell me,' said one, 'how's business?'

'Well, you know how it is,' the other replied. 'My life is like sex. When it's good it's wonderful – and when it's bad, it's still pretty good.'

HIS WATERLOO

A fellow visiting London asked a big bear of a taxi-driver where was the best place to find a piece of the action.

'Take the Underground to King's Cross, mate,' said the taxi-driver, 'and then just walk around – you'll very soon pick up something.'

The visitor got confused in the Underground, and ended up at Waterloo instead of King's Cross. But within five minutes he had made a pick-up and the girl brought him to a cosy little flat behind the station. He had just taken off his jacket and tie, when suddenly there was the sound of footsteps and then of a key being inserted in the door.

'Quick!' said the girl, 'get into the kitchen and start fiddling about with the sink. I'll tell my husband you're a plumber come to fix the tap.'

The man rushed into the kitchen just as the front door opened and the husband walked in. He had just turned on the taps and was trying hard to look like a plumber at work, when a gruff voice from the doorway said, 'Oh, it's you, is it? I thought I told you King's Cross.'

FOOTBALL FIELD

At a school football match a player collided with the goalpost and the other players quickly collected around him.

His recovery seemed to be taking a long time, so the teacher in charge came over.

'Now, what's going on here?' he demanded.

'We're trying to give him artificial respiration, sir,' said one of the boys. 'But he keeps getting up and walking away.'

FOOTBALL STADIUM

'I don't know what's the matter with me today,' muttered the centre-forward after missing the open goal. 'I'm not playing my usual game.'

'What game is that then, mate?' asked the opposing forward.

THE MOLECATCHER

In Manchester city at the sign of The Plough,
There lives a molecatcher and I can't tell you how.

He goes a-molecatching from morning to night,
And a young fellow comes there for to play with his wife.

Now the molecatcher, jealous of that very thing
He hid in the wash-house to watch him come in.

'Oh, where is your husband, my pretty dear?'
'He's gone a-molecatching, you need have no fear.'

She's gone up the stairs to give him the sign,
And the old molecatcher crept close up behind.

And the young fellow was in the midst of his frolics,
The molecatcher grabbed him quite fast by his . . . jacket.

Now the molecatcher cheered and he laughed to his wife,
'There's the biggest mole I ever caught in me life!

But I'll make him pay well for the ploughing o' me ground,
And the money it'll cost him no less than ten pound.'

'Well,' said the young fellow, 'the money I don't mind,
It only works out to about twopence a time.'

So come all you young fellows and mind what you're at,
Or else you'll get caught in the molecatcher's trap.

CAT'S-MEAT NELL

O that I in love, in love,
  In love had never fell;
I've tried in wain the heart to gain
  Of lovely Cat's-meat Nell.

'Twas in Drury lane, vere I
  First heard her voice so sweet,
As vith her barrow she vent by,
  And sweetly squalled 'Cat's meat!'
My heart she von; her swivel eyes
  So charmingly she roll'd,
And tempting her with 'Pies, hot pies!'
  My tale of love I told.

O that I in love, etc,

Elwated with liquor, I felt no dread,
  And thought as how I'd buss her,
For vich I catch'd a lick of the head,
  Vich made me summut the vorsser.
I look'd for I felt so stupid, do you see,
  To know vhere I vas, in wain,
To a butcher says I, 'I'm in Queer street.' Says he,
  'Why, you calf, this here is Cow lane.'

O that I in love, etc,

I never know'd in all my life,
    Faint heart fair lass e'er von,
So I, to try hard for a vife,
    Vith Nell again begun.
'Give me (said I) your kind embrace.'
    Says she, 'It's all a farce,
But if you will kiss, kiss away.'
    And she cocked up her bare arse.

    O that I in love, etc,

Says I, 'Nell, I'm in love, my dear,
    And wish to know if vether,
We to St Giles's church shall steer,
    And there be spliced together.'
Says she, 'Mr Pieman, it's no go,
    Vith me to talk of love,
A stinking pieman, you must know,
    I thinks myself above.'

    O that I in love, etc,

To Holborn then away jogg'd ve,
    Vhen I ax'd her to stop.
Says I, 'Nell, tho' you don't love me,
    Mayhaps you'd love a drop.
This here's The Bell, so let's toll in.'
    Says she, 'Yer gallous polite.'
And there ve took imperial gin,
    Till ve got muzzy quite.

    O that I in love, etc,

Close by her side I vent on, toddling,
   And, hot with love, kept chaffing,
While Nelly, vith her barrow vaddling,
   Set all the boys a-laughing.
The bother of those saucy brats
   Confus'd and cross'd our cries,
So, vile I call'd out, 'Hot mutton cats,'
   Vhy Nell she bawl'd 'Cat's pies!'

   O that I in love, etc,

In the Country

THE TRUCK-DRIVER'S HIGHWAY CODE

When should you use your headlights?
  To warn your mates of a speedtrap.

When do you overtake on the left?
  When the bastard in front won't move over.

What documents do you take on the road?
  Daily Mirror, Sun, Playboy and *Forum*.

When do you stop?
  To have a piss, leg over, or a tot of brandy.

Where should you not park?
  Outside the house of the tart you are screwing.

What would you expect to find on a rural road?
  Rural tarmac.

How many types of pedestrian crossings are there?
  Those who do and those that don't.

What is the correct procedure for overtaking on a motorway?
  Foot down hard, eyes shut, and smile.

When should you use the fast lane on a motorway?
  When you're going home on a promise.

What do you do in the event of a breakdown on the motorway?

Leave the fucking thing and hitch a lift home.

What does the yellow junction box mean?

They have run out of white paint.

What do broken white lines mean in the road?

Careless navvies.

When can you cross double white lines on the road?

After nine lagers, two vodkas and a whisky.

How do you avoid drowsiness on a motorway?

Finger your hitch-hiker.

What must you check before leaving a building site?

That you have enough timber under the sheet for a new kitchen cabinet.

What do double yellow lines on the side of a road mean?

Chinese take-away ahead.

Where do you situate your danger triangle when you break down?

Up the transport manager's arse.

YOU HAVE JUST PASSED THE H.G.V TEST.

FANCY FOOTWORK

Two men on a walking tour of the Scottish Highlands lost their way in an apparently uninhabited part of the mountains. They were still lost when the light began to fade.

At last they spotted a lonely cottage. They followed the path to the door and knocked. An attractive woman answered, and hearing their story, invited them to stay the night – she occasionally let rooms to tourists, and would be glad to put them up for the night and fix them a meal.

The next morning they resumed their tour.

About ten months later, they met up again. One said to the other, 'Oh Bill, I've been meaning to have a word with you. Do you remember when we were on holiday last year and we spent the night at that cottage in the mountains?'

'Yes, I do,' said Bill.

'Did you by any chance get up during the night and visit the bedroom of that personable widow who put us up?'

'Well, yes, I did.'

'And did you by any chance give her my name and address?'

'Er – well, yes, I did.'

'Well, it may interest you that I had a letter from her solicitors this morning, and . . . '

'Look here, Ted, I'm awfully sorry, but you know how it is . . . '

'Oh, don't apologise. I thought you'd like to know that she died last week and left me £20,000.'

IN A CAR

They were driving along a country lane.

The girl said, 'Oh, for heaven's sake, George, use both hands!'

George replied, 'I'd like to, darling, but I can't. I have to use one for steering.'

A LOT OF BULL

An elderly city couple made a visit to a farm. It happened on a day when the bull serviced three cows, one after the other. The couple watched in silence, but the wife seemed very impressed.

On the way home, she said to her husband, 'That bull wasn't content with one poor time, not *him*!'

And he replied, 'Nor with one poor cow, either.'

BAREFOOT GIRLS

A fellow made a long trip into the backwoods of Arkansas, USA, and when he got back he began to brag about all the pretty girls he'd laid up with along the road.

So finally an old-timer said, 'That ain't nothing to brag about, son. Everybody knows them Arkansas girls kind of lose their heads whenever they see a man that has got shoes on.'

FARMER'S AREN'T QUEER

Farmer: D'you hear about that book that's been written about us farmers?
Second farmer: What's it say about us?
Farmer: It says us farmers go around fucking sheep – and chickens – and snakes –
Second farmer: *Snakes?*

TWO CAN PLAY

A farmer who was shopping around for a new pick-up truck became thoroughly disgusted with the pricing system – everything was extra, mirrors, number plates, you name it. Eventually he settled on a purchase.

By coincidence, the dealer who sold him the truck came round to the farm a while later to buy a cow for his smallholding. The farmer quickly sized up the situation, and wrote out an itemised bill.

Basic cow	£1,000.00
Two-tone exterior	25.00
Extra stomach	75.00
Product storage compartment	35.00
Dispensing device (4 spigots @ £10 each)	40.00
Genuine cowhide upholstery	100.00
Automatic fly swatter	25.00
Dual horns	10.00
TOTAL (exclusive of VAT and delivery)	£1,310.00

COWBOYS AND SHERIFFS

A silence fell on the saloon bar when the sheriff pushed through the swing doors and walked slowly to the bar.

'Pour me a red-eye,' he says.

The barman poured the drink. The sheriff leaned towards him. 'I'm looking for the Brown-Paper Kid. Is he in here?'

The barman nodded towards a table where some men were playing poker. The sheriff downed his drink and walked over.

'Which one of you is the Brown-Paper Kid?'

'I am.'

'You got brown-paper britches?' asked the sheriff.

'Uh huh.'

'You got a brown-paper belt?'

'Uh huh.'

'You wear a brown-paper holster?'

'Yup.'

'You got a brown-paper hat?'

'Yes, I do.'

'You got brown-paper boots?'

'Yup.'

'Well, boy, I'm takin' you in.'

'What for, sheriff?'

'Rustlin.'

ENGLISH HISTORY BY MARK TWAIN

My, you ought to seen old Henry the Eighth when he was in bloom. He *was* a blossom. He used to marry a new wife every day, and chop off her head next morning. And he would do it just as indefferent as if he was ordering up eggs. 'Fetch up Nell Gwynn,' he says. They fetch her up. Next morning, 'Chop off her head' – and they chop it off. 'Fetch up Jane Shire,' he says; and up she comes. Next morning, 'Chop off her head' – and they chop it off. 'Ring up Fair Rosamun.' Fair Rosamun answers the bell. Next morning, 'Chop off her head.' And he made every one of them tell him a tale every night; and he kept that up till he had hogged a thousand and one tales that way, and then he put them all in a book, and called it Domesday Book – which was a good name and stated the case.

OLD HOLLYWOOD HITS RE-WORDED

The familiar song, 'Pardon me, boy, is this the Chatanooga choo-choo?' underwent a few changes.

Roy Rogers and Dale were in their little ranch home in the West. Roy was wearing brand new cowboy boots, but when he was out on the range, a huge puma suddenly pounced on him. He managed to escape with a mauling. Dale says: 'Pardon me, Roy, is that the cat that chewed your new shoe?'

Then there was the actor who played The Shadow. He had a Chinese houseboy, and one day when he returned from work, he finds the houseboy eating a sweet. He asks: 'Pardon me, Choy, is that The Shadow's nougat you chew?'

And, on the set of *The Thin Man*, Myrna Loy at last finds the right dress fabric for one of her scenes. William Powell says: 'Pardon me, Loy, is that the shantung that's the new clue?'

HEARING'S BELIEVING

In the days when soldiers on Continental campaigns were billeted in local farmhouses, they were often welcomed by the peasants' wives, if not by the peasants.

One soldier propositioned his landlady when her husband was away. He promised that they'd make a General between them, if she'd let him have her.

'A General!' she said, very impressed. 'All right, then.'

'But you must not fart,' he warned.

As it happened, he gave her such a thrust that she did fart.

'Oh dear,' he said. 'Instead of a General, it will only be a drummer.'

THE MAN WHO DID HIS WIFE'S WORK

A contrary man thought his wife didn't do enough work. He came back from haying and complained that he had all the hard work while she had an easy time. She said, very well, they would swop. He'd do her job, and she'd do his. She picked up the scythe and went out to the fields, and he started in on the household duties.

When his wife returned at the end of the day, he told her how he'd managed. First he took two shirts to the river to wash them, but they were carried away downstream, and while he went running after them, a goshawk took the hen and chickens, and the pig ate the millet and the dough.

'And what happened to the cream?' asked the wife, looking around.

'The cream? Oh, I spilt it all.'

'And what happened to your clothes?'

'When I went after the shirts, I left my clothes on the bank, and someone must have taken them. I had to make myself an apron of grass, but then, when I went to get back in the cart, the mare ate the apron.'

'And where is your member?'

'The mare ate that too.'

THE DEMONS

Astrologers warned a king that if his newborn son was to avoid an early death, he must not see sun nor light until he was grown. The baby was kept in an underground chamber, away from all interference, until then.

When it was safe, the lad was brought out and shown the wonders of the world: gold, silver, jewels, weapons, horses, carriages, robes. But it was the women who helped carry in the treasures who caught his attention. 'What are they?' he asked. He was told, 'They are the demons who lead men astray.'

When the king asked which of all the beautiful things he most desired, the boy replied, 'The demons who lead men astray.'

WRONG ROAD

The travelling salesman asked the farmer to put him up for the night. The farmer said, 'Certainly, but you'll have to sleep with my son.'

'Good Lord!' said the salesman. 'I'm in the wrong joke!'

GENERAL GUINNESS

You've heard of General Wellington who won at Waterloo,
But there's a good old Irishman I'll mention unto you.
He comes from dear old Dublin, he's a man we all applaud,
For he always finds a corkscrew far more handy than a sword.

He's good old General Guinness,
He's a soldier strong and 'stout',
Found at every 'bottle-front',
And he can't be done without.
His noble name has world-wide fame,
For every heart he cheers,
Good old General Guinness of the country's booseliers.

This hale and hearty warrior is worshipped in the ranks.
He does his task inside the cask as well as in the tanks.
And he bears the brunt on every front, north, south, east and west,
And he wears about ten thousand canteen medals on his chest.

He's good old General Guinness,
He's won the world's applause
For it's he who kept our spirits up
In the midst of all the wars.
Who was the first to flirt with
Mademoiselle from Armentières?
Why, good old General Guinness of the country's booseliers.

All over Bonnie Scotland too the General is seen,
They've given him the freedom of the town of Aberdeen.
From Inverness to Galashiels he keeps them warm and bright,
They love to gather round him och on every moonlit night.

    He's good old General Guinness,
    He's as good as Scottish broth,
    'Twas he who turned the Firth of Forth
    Into the Firth of Froth.
    All Scotsmen dance the Highland Fling
    And shout when he appears,
    Hurrah for General Guinness and the country's booseliers!

Abroad

WILDCAT STRIKE IN ANCIENT EGYPT!!!!

The Union of Eunuchs and Sopranos Strikes!
In a dispute about severance pay.

IN ANCIENT ROME

While Thersander was away in Gaul with his legion, he believed that his wife Melita was having an affair with Quintus, a long-time admirer of hers. When Thersander got home, he questioned her about it. She denied it vehemently, but he eventually insisted that Melita must undergo the trial of the River Styx.

This was the ancient test for wives suspected of infidelity. It required that the wife must walk into the river. The river would fall back before an irreproachable woman, but would rise above the head of one who had been evil.

Melita entered the river, and the water fell away.

She was wearing around her neck a tablet on which was her oath that all the time her husband was gone, she had never been intimate with Quintus.

(This was because she wasn't, until after her husband returned.)

THE TAMING OF THE SHREW

There lived a Moor who was much respected and who had a son, the most promising youth in the world. There also lived another Moor who was very much richer and who had an only daughter of so violent a temper that no one would marry her. But the young man sought to enrich himself by such a marriage.

So they were married and the bride taken home; the friends and relations waited anxiously for the following day.

The young couple sat down to supper, when the bridegroom saw the mastiff and said to him, 'Bring me water wherewith to wash my hands.'

The dog naturally taking no notice of the command, the young man arose in a great rage, and drawing his sword, commenced a savage attack upon the dog and cut off its head.

Thus furious and blood-stained he returned to the table and saw a cat. 'Bring me water for my hands,' said he.

The animal not noticing the command, the master cried out, 'How, false traitor, do you not see how I treated the mastiff for disobeying me? If you do not do as I tell you this instant you shall share his fate.'

The poor cat continuing motionless, the master seized him by his paws and dashed him against the wall.

His fury increasing, he espied his horse and called to it fiercely to bring him water. The animal not obeying, he cried out, 'How is this? Think you that because you are the only horse I have that you dare thus to disobey my orders?' Saying this, he cut off its head.

He sat down to table, swearing he would kill a thousand horses, or men or women, if they disobeyed him. He looked around and ordered his wife to bring him water. She immediately rose and brought it to him.

Thus passed the night; she not daring to speak but strictly obeying all his orders. After letting her sleep for a short time he said, 'Get up, take care that nothing disturbs me.'

The following morning, the relatives came stealthily to the door. She went cautiously towards them and exclaimed, 'Traitors, what are you doing? Speak not – be silent or all of us are dead!'

They were much astonished, and on learning what had taken place, they esteemed the young man very much who had made so good a commencement in the management of his household. From that day his wife became tractable and compliant, so they led a very happy life.

A few days later his father-in-law likewise killed a horse in order to intimidate his wife.

But she said to him, 'My friend, it is too late to begin now; it would not avail you to kill a hundred horses! We know each other too well.'

IN OLD RUSSIA

A Russian priest and his wife went off to a wedding, leaving their daughter at home with the serving-man. He proposed that they eat two cooked suckling pigs left in the house, and she agreed.

So they ate one. 'As to the other' he said, 'I will hide it under your gown, so that it will not be found, and a little later we will eat it also. If they question us about the pigs, we will both reply that the cat ate them.'

'But how will you hide it under my gown?'

'That is not your business. I know how.'

So he tucked up her dress and put his yard into her.

'Ah, you hide it very well, but how shall I get it out of there?'

'Be easy. You have only to show it some hay, and it will come out of its own accord.'

He had in fact trussed her so well that she became pregnant. When the child moved, she thought it was the pig. She lifted up her leg, spread some hay on the ground, and called, 'Tchoukh, tchoukh, tchoukh!' It will come out perhaps, she thought, if I call if thus.

By the time her parents had asked her about her big stomach, and she explained it was a little pig which the serving-man had put there, the man had taken care to disappear.

THE GIRL WHO WAS KIND TO WOMEN

In China, a prince persuaded his tutor to find a woman for him. The tutor set up a tent in the woods by the road. He told the prince to lie down on the bed inside it, and to cover himself carefully.

Then the tutor walked forward to meet a procession he had seen in the distance. A rich farmer was bringing his very young daughter to her betrothed. The tutor beseeched him to allow his daughter to help his own young wife who, he said, had been overtaken with the pains of childbirth. The father thought this would be a good omen for his child's forthcoming marriage, and agreed. He sent attendants to accompany her to the tent.

They followed the tutor, and as they went along he begged the little girl to let him know as soon as the child was delivered if it was a boy or a girl.

She went into the tent, lifted the covers, and cried in confusion, 'It is a boy! It *is* a boy!'

The prince covered her with kisses until she was silent. After a brief stay, the pretty little traveller came out of the hut. The tutor asked her, 'Was it really a boy?'

She replied, 'It was indeed,' and with her attendants went back in the procession to her bridegroom.

THE MAN WHO HAD A BABY

There was a judge in Syria who gave sentences with the utmost penalties, and who kept only one servant, an old woman, because of his stinginess. Though he was very rich, he lived on stale bread and onions, but he liked to be thought generous. If anyone called at meal-time, the judge would cry to his servant, 'Lay the gold-fringed cloth!' But no meal was ever served.

'Lay the gold-fringed cloth' became a proverb. A man who had been skimped at a feast would say 'I ate at the judge's gold-fringed cloth.'

Nonetheless, people who hoped to benefit from his judgement cultivated him. One of them said, 'Oh judge, I have a very beautiful daughter. I would be greatly honoured if you would make her your wife.'

The judge accepted and the marriage took place at once. The girl was brought to his house and being sweet and amiable, made no comment when no food was produced. The guests stayed on hopefully, but finally gave up and went home.

The young wife had begun to starve before she heard her husband tell the servant to lay the gold-fringed cloth, but she could not manage to swallow the stale bread and onion and left the table. After three days of this menu she sent for her father to take her away. The judge was furious. Cursing her, he cut off her hair, accused her of all vices, divorced her, and threw her out on the street.

A short time later he married again. But the same thing happened – the girl was starved, shorn and divorced. He then married another, with the same result. And another, and another, and another. This gave rise to much talk, and the matrons banded together and decreed that the miser was to be considered unmarriageable.

Now that no one would have him, the judge decided

he wanted marriage very much. After some time passed, he was delighted when he saw a beautiful woman riding by who cast a glance at him.

'Are you married or single?' he asked.

'Single,' said she.

'Will you marry me?' asked the judge.

'I will marry you if you will give me a dowry of fifty dinars,' she replied.

The next day he forced himself to produce the money, and they were duly married in the presence of witnesses, but the witnesses went away unfed.

'Lay the gold-fringed cloth,' cried the judge, and the servant set the bread and onions. The new bride took her portion and ate it with smiles. 'I thank Allah for this excellent repast,' she said.

Next morning when the judge went to preside at the court, the new bride inspected the house. In one room there was a big cabinet, well locked and barred with iron. She walked around it many times, looking closely, and noticed a small hole in one of the carvings that almost would admit a finger. Setting her eye to it, she was overjoyed to see a great treasure of gold and silver pieces overspilling from jars on the floor inside. She smeared some glue on the end of a palm stem and managed to get it into the cabinet and out again with several gold pieces sticking to it. Returning to her own room, she called the old servant and gave her the money. 'Go out to the market,' she said, 'and buy fresh rolls, and rice, and tender lamb, and the finest fruits and pastries you can find.'

When the servant returned, the girl made her join in the meal, and the old woman wept with joy. 'You may feed like this every day,' the bride told her, 'if only you will keep silence and say nothing to the judge.'

'Lay the gold-fringed cloth!' cried the judge when he returned that noon, but his wife served him with the remains of her feast. He ate till he could hold no more. 'But where did you get this?' he asked.

'Dear husband,' said she, 'I have many relatives in this city and one of them sent these dishes to me.'

The next day, an even more expensive meal was served, and the bride explained that an aunt had sent it. The judge congratulated himself on having chosen such a well-related wife.

At the end of a year, the judge had developed a belly that became famous. He did not know that his wife had married him to avenge all the girls he had starved and cast aside.

One of the women she fed every day was the pregnant wife of a poor porter who already had five children. The judge's wife asked her if she would give the next baby to her, as she was barren. She would care for it as her own. But she must do it secretly and tell no one. The porter's wife was happy to agree. A baby boy was born soon after, and the judge's wife received him.

That very next day she prepared a dish of beans, peas, lentils, cabbages, onions, garlic, various heavy grains and many spices. The judge took helping after helping of this and proclaimed it his favourite dish. But very shortly his belly began to swell. Noises were heard inside him like thunder, like a tempest! He rolled on the floor and screamed for help, and his wife rubbed his stomach. Suddenly she said, 'Oh, oh, a miracle!'

'What miracle?' he cried, 'Help, oh help!'

'Exalted be the name of the Highest!' she called out, 'His will be done! Oh, husband, you are with child! And your time is close at hand!'

A terrible pain convulsed the judge. He howled and heaved, and let out a tremendous fart like an earthquake which shook the foundations of the house and threw the judge forward so that he fainted.

When he came to himself, he saw a little mattress by

his side and on it a new-born baby. His wife was bent over him, saying, 'Praise be to Allah for a happy deliverance!' and the judge, relieved of pain, now believed in this miraculous birth.

'Surely Allah can bring forth children according to his will,' he told himself. 'Even a man may bear a child! Get me a nurse, dear wife, for I cannot feed him.'

'I had already thought of that; one is waiting. But are you sure you have no milk?'

The judge felt anxiously and answered, 'No, there is nothing there.

The wife was delighted with the success of her strategy, and telling the judge that he must stay in bed for forty days and nights, she gave him medicines, and he fell asleep, worn out by his colic. But when he woke, his mind as well as his body was ill at ease.

His first concern was to enjoin secrecy on his wife. 'I am lost forever if folk get to know that the judge has given birth!'

Instead of reassuring him she replied, 'We are not the only ones who know of the fortunate miracle. All our neighbours have already heard about it from the nurse. They are all babblers.'

The judge spent the forty days racked by worry. 'Surely my foes will accuse me of ridiculous things!' he said to himself. 'They will think that I have let myself be buggered in some extraordinary way, and that it is all very well for me to be severe in my judgements when I have myself been up to such strange immoralities!'

The more he thought, the more dismal his case appeared. Finally he resolved to leave the city rather than be recognised in the streets. He told his wife. While pretending deep sorrow that he would have to leave his high office, she made him even more determined to flee.

'Evil tongues are certainly wagging about you now,' she said. 'But it will all soon be forgotten. You can return and devote yourself to rearing your child.' That very night the judge crept out of the house and started on the road to Damascus.

He arrived weary but relieved by the thought that no one knew his name or his story. Yet in the next few days he heard the tale of his exploit repeated countless times in public places. Happily, no one knew his face, and he was able to go his way.

Though he existed in an even more miserly way than before, after some time his money ran out. Rather than send a message to his wife which would have to reveal where his treasure was kept, he hired himself out as a mortar-carrier.

Years went by, and the old judge had become as thin as a cat. At last, feeling certain that time had erased the memory of his misfortune, he returned to his native city. As he went through the gate, he saw a group of children playing and heard one of them saying to another, 'You can't expect to win, because you were born in the judge's year, the year of the Father of Farts.'

'I thank Allah,' thought the delighted judge, 'that another judge has caused my tale to be forgotten!'

He went up to the boy who had spoken and asked, 'What judge is the one whom you call the Father of Farts?'

'He was given that name,' answered the child, 'because once when he had broken wind enormously, his wife made him think . . .'

The judge didn't wait for more. Realising for the first time how he had been fooled, he ran to his own house. But it was open to the wind, the roof and floors were broken, the walls had crumbled. In the remains of his treasure cabinet there was not even one coin. His neighbours heard his loud lament and told him that his wife had given him up for dead and departed with all his goods to a distant country. They could not help laughing.

Without a word, he turned and left. Nothing was ever heard of him again.

IN OLD TIME FRANCE

Lise was a young French girl who had always been told that she lacked wit. She doesn't know how to get it. She confides in the priest, Father Bonaventure, who generously supplies her with some of his.

She tells her friend Nanette about this and asks how Nanette got her wit.

'From your brother,' Nanette replies.

Lise is very surprised. 'He hasn't any; how could he give it to you?'

And in an old-time *diligence* in Picardy, as crowded as a modern bus, a young lady was forced to sit on a peasant's lap.

'Remove your cane!' she ordered.

A very young nun in a French convent painted a picture of the infant Jesus as a gift from the nuns to the Superior. The nuns all laughed at it but wouldn't say why.

The young nun asked Jan, the gardener, who explained that she had made the infant female. But he said he would model for her.

This was arranged. She worked hard. The sweat rolled down.

Afterwards she called in the other nuns for a second viewing. 'Ah,' they exclaimed. 'That's Jan's!'

FROM THE EAST

A perverse and cunning man named Zubair had a beautiful wife who did not love him. She loved another man, and he loved her, but these two were unable to meet.

Next door to Zubair's house was the home of a learned man who used to lecture every evening on history and philosophy to whoever gathered there to hear him. Now the sage also had a beautiful wife, and the lover of Zubair's wife pretended, for his own reasons, to be smitten with her, although she was in fact very virtuous and dearly loved her husband.

This is what the lover planned: after seeking out Zubair and swearing him to secrecy, he told him he was in love with the sage's wife. He asked Zubair to help him with this intrigue. Zubair said the woman would never agree. 'Ah,' cried the lover, 'it is impossible for me to renounce her. My fortune is large; expense is no object. I will give you two ounces of silver every day on condition that you go each evening to listen to your neighbour's lecture, and as soon as he has finished, to speak to him in a loud voice. When I hear you, I will know the husband has finished.'

Zubair agreed. So while he carried out his agreement at the sage's house, the other joined the woman of his choice and delighted with her until the end of the lecture.

As soon as Zubair began to shout at the sage, the lover left his mistress, and Zubair did not for a moment suspect.

But after several evenings the sage began to think it strange that Zubair should always speak out so loudly when he was on the point of ending. On the next occasion, he closed his discourse much sooner than usual and, seizing Zubair, cried 'As Allah lives, if you say a single word I'll break your bones!'

Then he dragged Zubair into his wife's room, where she was quietly occupied with some domestic work. The sage thought for a moment and then dragged Zubair along the balcony to the neighbouring house. The wife followed, and all three saw the wife of Zubair in a fine position with her lover.

The sage said, 'Oh wicked and unhappy Zubair, the dishonour is yours, and you yourself opened the door for it!'

In shame, Zubair repudiated his wife and left the country.

THE RAJAH OF ASTRAKHAN

There was a Rajah of Astrakhan,
A most licentious kind of man,
Of wives he had a hundred and nine,
Including his favourite concubine.

One day when there was no one at hand
He called a eunuch, one of his band,
'Go down to my harem, you lazy swine,
And fetch my favourite concubine.'

The eunuch fetched the concubine,
A figure like Venus, a face divine.
The Rajah gave a significant grunt,
And placed himself within her . . . arms.

The Rajah bellowed loud and long,
The maiden answered sure and strong.
But just when all had come to a head,
They both fell off the royal bed.

They hit the floor with a hell of a crack
Which completely ruined the poor girl's back.
And as for the Rajah's magnificent end,
It split down the middle and started to bend.

There is a moral to this tale,
There is a moral to this tale,
If you would try a girl at all
Stick her right up against the wall.

The Pearly Gates

FAIR . . .

Abie was busy praying that he would win £10,000 on his premium bond.

The first week, winners were announced but there was nothing for Abie.

Abie prayed harder than ever. 'Please, God, let me win a prize on the premium bond!'

The next week, nothing happened.

Abie prayed and prayed. 'Let me win a prize!'

But the next week, still nothing.

So Abie decided he was through with it all. 'What's the good of praying,' he asked God, 'if You never let me win?'

Then God said, 'Abie, meet me halfway! At least buy a premium bond!'

St Peter, at the Pearly Gates, was interviewing a new arrival.
St Peter: Name?
New arrival: Leroy.
St Peter: While you were on earth, did you ever steal, lie, cheat, or swear?
Leroy: No.
St Peter: Did you ever gamble, drink, or smoke?
Leroy: No.
St Peter: Were you ever promiscuous?
Leroy: Oh, no!
St Peter: Tell me, what kept you so long?

PARDON

A famous surgeon died and went to heaven.

'There's just one thing I'd like to get off my mind before I'm admitted,' he said to the saint at the Gates. 'I used to play football for the St Bart's team, and one afternoon when we were playing against Guy's Hospital, I scored a goal that I knew was offside, but the referee didn't notice and it was allowed. That goal won us the match. I suppose it's not very important, St Peter, but even after all these years, I still feel guilty.'

'Oh, don't worry about that,' said the saint cheerfully. 'We know all about it, and it's quite OK as far as we're concerned.'

'Thank you for that good news!' The surgeon sighed with relief.

'By the way,' added the saint, opening the Gates, 'my name's not St Peter. It's St Bartholomew.'

HEAVEN?

In Heaven, a Christian and a Jew spent all their time arguing.

The Jew said, 'Your whole religion is based on ours, anyway. Why, you even took the Ten Commandments from us!'

'We may have taken them,' said the Christian, 'but you certainly can't say that we kept them.'

COLD COMFORT

A very rich and proud princess from one of Europe's oldest families died at the age of ninety-three.

St Peter welcomed her at the Gates, and before he could question her, she gave him her genealogy in great detail and at greater length. She showed him some very expensive old family jewels which she'd managed to bring with her. Finally, she unpacked a bag and produced photographs framed in gold that showed her with several crowned heads.

St Peter shook his head sadly. 'Come in here, by all means,' he said. 'But I think you'll be lonely.'

HELL

In an after-dinner speech, a Brigadier General told how he'd fallen asleep while reading Dante's *The Divine Comedy* which tells of a tour through Hell, Purgatory and Heaven. The Italian poet had as his guide for part of the trip the classic Roman poet, Virgil.

The General said that he'd dreamed he had made the same journey. Virgil was guiding him, but they'd gone to Heaven first. Here, Virgil had pointed out that the English were the police, the French were the cooks, the Germans played the music, the Italians were the lovers and the Swiss were the managers.

'Then,' said the General, 'we went to Hell. And in Hell, the English were the cooks, the French played the music, the Germans were the police, the Swiss were the lovers and the Italians were the managers.'

Everyone laughed.

And the General added, 'When Virgil heard this, he left! And I did too – I woke up.'

FAILED

An Anglican, a Methodist and a Catholic were all waiting – in Heaven's car showroom. St Peter was to assign them their transport, the standard of which was related to how well they had behaved during their lives.

St Peter asked each one of them in turn only one question. 'How many women have you slept with?'

The Methodist said, 'Only one – my wife.'

'Excellent!' said St Peter. 'You can have a Rolls Royce.'

The Anglican had slept with three. He got a BMW.

The Catholic couldn't remember how many he'd slept with. He got a Ford, and drove off, dejected.

But a few minutes later, he was back, laughing hard.

'What's the matter with you, you old lecher?' asked the Methodist.

'Well,' he replied. 'I was just driving down the road when I saw the Pope – riding a bicycle!'

FAILED AGAIN!

A businessman was at the Pearly Gates, seeking admission.

'What have you done that entitles you to come in?' asked St Peter.

'Well, the other day I saw an old woman in rags on Oxford Street, and I gave her 10p in coppers.'

'Gabriel!' called St Peter. 'Is that on the records?'

'Yes, Peter,' answered Gabriel, 'it's all here.'

'What else have you done?' continued St Peter.

'I was waiting for the bus last year, when an old beggar with his clothes in tatters came by. He was nearly frozen with the cold, so I gave him 20p.'

'Gabriel, is that in the records?'

'Yes, St Peter, it's down here.'

'What else have you done?'

'Well, I can't think of anything else just at the moment . . .'

'Gabriel! What shall we do with him?'

'Give him back his 30p . . .'

'What!' cried St Peter.

'. . . and tell him to go to Hell.'

33⅓% PURE

An Englishman, an Irishman and a Scotsman are being warned by St Peter that their wings will fall off if they have any impure thoughts.

Just then a beautiful blonde squeezes past the Scotsman, and his wings fall off.

The Irishman bends down to pick them up. And the Englishman's wings fall off.

A GOOD DOZEN

Twelve wives arrived at the Pearly Gates.

'Now, ladies,' said the officiating angel. 'How many of you have been unfaithful to your husbands?'

Eleven ladies blushed and put up their hands.

'OK,' sighed the angel, picking up the telephone. 'Hello, is that Hell? Do you have room for twelve unfaithful wives, one of them stone deaf?'

YOU ARE ABOUT TO ENTER HEAVEN

Just outside the Pearly Gates, on the nearest cloud, is a luxurious double-bed with a lovely girl lying on it, stark naked and holding a sign that says 'LAST CHANCE!'

HELL FROM NOW ON

At the Pearly Gates, a rich man was checked carefully and then sent firmly to Hell.

He was deeply ashamed by this. 'But at least,' he thought, 'no one in Hell knows me.' So he began to look around, and to his great embarrassment, practically the first person who spotted him was his old valet, John.

'Good afternoon, sir,' said John. 'What are you doing here? A man as generous and popular as you, should surely have gone to Heaven!'

'Ah, my good old John,' said the man. 'I was sent here because I cheated my tenants and defrauded my family in order to pay the debts of that rascal, my son, the apple of my eye! But you, John, what's an honest fellow like you doing here?'

'For begetting that son,' said the valet sadly.

TRY HELL INSTEAD

Three sinners were waiting anxiously at the Gates of Hell, when one of them began to complain.

'It's outrageous,' said he. 'I never drank, or smoked, although I did commit adultery once or twice. There's no way I should be here!'

'Well,' said the second, 'I never drank or committed adultery, either. There's no way I should be here!'

The third was less confident. 'Unfortunately, I was an atheist, and so I got drunk every night, slept around, and generally had a damned good time.'

At this moment the Devil opened the gate to Hell and grinned at the third man. 'C'mon,' he said, 'let's burn those two bores and go out for a drink.'

BEELZEBUB

There was an old man lived on a farm,
Hi ho dan do,
There was an old man lived on a farm,
But he hadn't no cattle to carry it on.

   Chorus: 'Twas fi do, fi diddle, fi dum fi day.

Old Devil come to him in the field one day,
Hi ho dan do,
Old Devil come to him in the field one day,
Says, 'One of your family I'll carry away.'

'You can't have my oldest son,
Hi ho dan do,
You can't have my oldest son,
For his hard work has just now begun.

But you can have my scolding wife,
Hi ho dan do,
But you can have my scolding wife,
For we never could agree in our life.'

He picked her up all on his back,
Hi ho dan do,
He picked her up all on his back,
I never seen a pedlar so ashamed of his pack.

Two little devils come with the chains,
Hi ho dan do,
Two little devils come with the chains,
With a blow of her fist she knocked out their brains.

Two little devils says, 'Hold her up higher!'
Hi ho dan do,
Two little devils says, 'Hold her up higher!'
She up with her foot and kicked nine in the fire.

Two little devils peeped over the wall,
Hi ho dan do,
Two little devils peeped over the wall,
Says, 'Take her back, daddy, she a-killing us all!'

The next she met was Beelzebub,
Hi ho dan do,
The next she met was Beelzebub,
She knocked him down with the devil of a club.

He picked her up all on his back,
Hi ho dan do,
He picked her up all on his back,
And like a fool went a-packing her back.

When she got near home she gave a big yell,
Hi ho dan do,
When she got near home she gave a big yell,
She swore she'd whipped all the devils in hell.

When she got there her man was lying in bed,
Hi ho dan do,
When she got there her man was lying in bed,
She picked up a plate and hammered his head.

Beelzebub went a-whistling over the hill,
Hi ho dan do,
Beelzebub went a-whistling over the hill,
If the devil won't have you, I don't know who will.

Get on yer bike!

GOB
Goods On Board

The hilarious new novel by
SIMON MAYLE

Dear Reader,

I promise you that this book is so witty you'll be reading it
aloud to the nearest traffic warden. You'll need three boxes of
extra-strong hankies for the sad bits. You'll find brilliant new
insights into modern romance.

Besides all this, there's a load of great stuff about motor-
cycling, Life, and what it's like to wear leather.

Basically, reading this is nearly as good as doing a ton down
the South Circular, or a wheelie along the Mall. Go for it!

James

0 7221 5750 9   GENERAL FICTION   £2.50

HENRY ROOT'S

A–Z of Women

'The Definitive Guide'

I know what you're thinking. You're thinking: Women, eh? What's there to say about women? The bedroom and the kitchen. The duvet and the blender. The corset and the rubber glove. That covers it, you're thinking. But Root on women, that's different…that's very different indeed.

So to balance the current spate of books by women on men, the incomparable Henry Root has gone out in the field and up at the sharp end – and has come back with the ultimate guide to women today.

0 7221 3067 8   Humour   £2.50

SHEATH-BURSTING ROMANCE!!!

BRUTE!

MALCOLM BENNETT & AIDAN HUGHES

BRUTE!
Colossal, work-hardened men! Wild untameable women!
Savage, unbridled passion! Raw and erotic tales of
gut-wrenching drama and suspense!!

BRUTE!
Romance, cruelty and religion! Sport, crime and agriculture!
Horror, western and football!!

BRUTE!
The cult comic of the 80s now unleashed in paperback!

'Unmatched in contemporary British comic art'
CITY LIMITS

'Tough and dirty' **THE FACE**

'Graphic, gruesome and hilarious' **BLITZ**

'In future all novels will be written like this' **TIME OUT**

0 7221 1565 2   CULT/GENERAL FICTION   £1.95

AMERICA'S SUPERSTAR STORYTELLER . . .

LAWRENCE SANDERS

TALES OF THE WOLF

When it comes to writing bestselling thrillers, no one does it better than Lawrence Sanders. With over 25 million copies of his books in print, Lawrence Sanders is the No. 1 master of suspense . . .

Now Sanders has created his most intriguing character since Edward X. Delaney. Meet Wolf Lannihan. Lannihan is an antihero who always gets what he wants – whether it's cracking an unsolvable case or making love to an unbelievable woman. Now Wolf is telling all . . . action-packed, nonstop tales that will keep you guessing right to the finish. Wolf guarantees it!

0 7221 7617 1   ADVENTURE THRILLER   £2.50

FICTION

BIRTHRIGHT	Joseph Amiel	£3.50 ☐
TALES OF THE WOLF	Lawrence Sanders	£2.50 ☐
MALIBU SUMMER	Stuart Buchan	£2.95 ☐
THE SECRETS OF HARRY BRIGHT	Joseph Wambaugh	£2.95 ☐
CYCLOPS	Clive Cussler	£3.50 ☐

FILM AND TV TIE-IN

INTIMATE CONTACT	Jacqueline Osborne	£2.50 ☐
BEST OF BRITISH	Maurice Sellar	£8.95 ☐
SEX WITH PAULA YATES	Paula Yates	£2.95 ☐
RAW DEAL	Walter Wager	£2.50 ☐

NON-FICTION

SOLDIERS	John Keegan & Richard Holmes	£5.95 ☐
URI GELLER'S FORTUNE SECRETS	Uri Geller	£2.50 ☐
A TASTE OF LIFE	Julie Stafford	£3.50 ☐
HOLLYWOOD A' GO-GO	Andrew Yule	£3.50 ☐
THE OXFORD CHILDREN'S THESAURUS		£3.95 ☐

All Sphere books are available at your local bookshop or newsagent, or can be ordered direct from the publisher. Just tick the titles you want and fill in the form below.

Name _____

Address _____

_____

Write to Sphere Books, Cash Sales Department, P.O. Box 11, Falmouth, Cornwall TR10 9EN

Please enclose a cheque or postal order to the value of the cover price plus:

UK: 60p for the first book, 25p for the second book and 15p for each additional book ordered to a maximum chrge of £1.90.

OVERSEAS & EIRE: £1.25 for the first book, 75p for the second book and 28p for each subsequent title ordered.

BFPO: 60p for the first book, 25p for the second book plus 15p per copy for the next 7 books, thereafter 9p per book.

Sphere Books reserve the right to show new retail prices on covers which may differ from those previously advertised in the text elsewhere, and to increase postal rates in accordance with the P.O.